YOU VE GOT THIS!

The Grad's Guide to the Big, Rich, Magnificent Life You Deserve

DINA MAURO

Printed in the United States of America
First Printing, 2017

ISBN-10: 0-9883782-2-1
ISBN-13: 978-0-9883782-2-3

Library of Congress Control Number: 2016920183

Editor: Kimberly Smith Ashley
www.KMSmithWrites.com

Book Cover & Layout: Summer R. Morris
www.SumoDesignStudio.com

Contents

A Letter to My Sons

Preface

Part One   **Starting Down the Path**   1

Chapter 1   You Are Magnificent   3

Chapter 2   Harnessing the Power of Your Mind   8

Chapter 3   Tapping into Mindfulness   11

Chapter 4   Staying in Your Lane   14

Chapter 5   Remaining Positive and Confident   17

Chapter 6   Unlocking the Magnificent You   24

Chapter 7   When You Feel Frustrated, Angry, or Grumpy   28

Chapter 8   When Victimhood Creeps In   31

Chapter 9   How to Ignore the Noise in Your Head   35

Chapter 10   Accepting a Compliment   38

Chapter 11   Taking Good Care of You   40

Part Two   **Hitting a Bump in the Road**   45

Chapter 12   When a Setback or Failure Happens   47

Chapter 13   Facing Those Hard-to-Get-out-of-Bed Mornings   50

Chapter 14   Learning from Mistakes   52

Chapter 15   What about Making Money?   55

Chapter 16   What about What Others Think?   58

Chapter 17   When the Pain Gets Real   60

Chapter 18   What about the "Addiction Gene"?   64

Chapter 19   When People Are Mean   67

Chapter 20   Four Steps to Overcome Rejection   71

Chapter 21   Regaining Perspective   74

Part Three   **Traveling with Others**   79

Chapter 22   Why Kindness Matters   81

Chapter 23   Family: A Deep and Sometimes Complicated Love   83

Chapter 24   Noting What You're Doing and Who You're With   87

Chapter 25   Introverts and Extroverts: Both Are Magnificent!   90

Chapter 26   When You Feel Lonely   93

Chapter 27   Making Someone's Day   97

Chapter 28   When Someone Is Grieving   99

Chapter 29   Navigating a Room Mostly Filled with Strangers   102

Chapter 30   How You Fit into the Workforce: It's Not All about IQ   106

Chapter 31   When You "Get" to Speak to an Audience   111

Chapter 32   You Get What You Give   114

Chapter 33   Is He (or She) the One?   116

Chapter 34   Why Can't Everyone Be Like Me? A Note on Tolerance   120

Part Four   **Loving the Magnificent Journey**   125

Chapter 35   Life Is about Courage   127

Chapter 36   Sacrifices: Squeezing the Balloon   130

Chapter 37   Challenge Yourself and Have a Plan   134

Chapter 38	Twelve Tips for Holding onto Happiness	137
Chapter 39	Three Tips for Managing Worry	140
Chapter 40	Out of the Nest and Certainly Not Falling: Nine Tips for College Freshman	143
Chapter 41	Ten Ways to Get Through Your First Day, Week, and Month on the Job	147
Chapter 42	Decision-Making 101	152
Chapter 43	Technology and Unsocial Media	155
Chapter 44	Tips and Tricks to Avoid Procrastination	159
Chapter 45	What a Magnificent Mess! Staying Neat and Organized	162
Chapter 46	Knowing What's Important and Good	167
Chapter 47	You Are Anything But Ordinary	171

Final Thoughts

About the Author

A LETTER TO MY SONS

Dear Owen, Ethan, and Aiden,

When each of you was born, your father and I sat alone in the hospital room staring at your fresh pink cheeks and sparse hair. We marveled at how handsome you were and wondered about the man you'd each become. You were a magical gift, and we couldn't wait to watch you flourish. We didn't yet know your individual personalities, but we did know you could enjoy a magnificent life and accomplish anything you wanted.

Like a small, anonymous seed in our hands, we couldn't tell if you were a palm tree, a rose bush, or a towering oak. We did know that our job was to nurture you so that you could become the best at *being you*. If you were a palm tree, we wanted you to be tall and strong. If you were a rose bush, we hoped you'd have vibrant flowers that attracted bees from miles away. If you were a towering oak, we craved for you to have massive limbs and a strong root system for when the winds of life came barreling against you.

Ethan, you have a zest for life, a spark in your eyes, and a knack for gabbing. I will always remember when you were rambling on as a toddler. Sometimes, even you couldn't figure out what you were trying to say, so you would end by saying, "I don't know what I talkin' about," and then you'd waddle away shaking your head in comical frustration. Hold tight and don't ever lose that sparkle, that marvelous shine in your green eyes. You are wicked smart, creative, charismatic, and can socialize with anyone. *What many gifts you have.*

Aiden, I will never forget your five-month-old, adorable, handsome round face when it pushed through the zip-up cover we put on your carrier to keep you warm. You had a silly and accomplished grin. You've always been headstrong, feisty, and determined. You've continually kept up with your older brothers and their friends, even on our incredibly long and difficult family hikes. Somehow, you always find a way to put one tiny determined foot in front of the other. Not many people are as gritty and unwavering as you are. When you direct that energy and use it to your advantage, you are a marvel to watch. *You don't give up, which means anything you want is within your reach.*

Owen, you are my responsible, funny, and dependable boy. I would follow you anywhere. As long as I can remember, you had humorous and unique names for our family members and pets. You renamed our yellow lab Driscoll "Rick Pick," and you affectionately call your brother Aiden "Bettlehump." Now "Bettlehump" is programmed into our home phone, so the name is broadcast every time Aiden calls. You've created so many fun nicknames that now they've become an inside family joke. For your entire life, you've kept unwavering morals, held high standards for yourself, and practiced relentless drive. You get things done. You make us laugh. *You are solid as a rock.*

Over the years, I've seen the three of you grow into young men, and I couldn't be prouder. Look in the mirror. My hope is that you see what I see—someone capable of anything you set out to accomplish, happiness and fulfillment at the ready. I know that at times it may be hard to believe that you are magnificent, but this awareness should be at the top of your list. Love yourself. There is no greater triumph.

I am honored to be your mother. When you were a child and I joined your class party, I couldn't wait for another mom to ask me which son was mine. When you played a sport, I begged for another parent to ask which player I was supporting. When we ran errands together, I hoped to bump into a colleague so that they would see the exceptional son next to me.

Now you're growing older. As much as I would like it, I won't always be here, but I'll always be with you within these pages. I've kept notes on what I've learned through the years, knowing that one day I would want to pass along these lessons to you. My hope is this will be a lifelong resource for you in times of struggle, when you need a little boost, or when you just aren't sure which way to go.

Navigating life can be thrilling and confusing. Sometimes, it's a matter of trial and error. I hope these words will inspire you to continue to be the incredible and mighty person you are and dig deep to strive for what you, and everyone on this earth, deserve—*a magnificent life.*

Stand before the looking glass, take a deep breath, and smile at the marvelous soul in front of you. That, my son, is what I've always seen.

All my love,
Mom

YOU'VE GOT THIS!

PREFACE

Congratulations, you've graduated! You may feel exhilarated about what's to come, or it may seem as though you're standing on the edge of a cliff, trying not to look down. Both emotions are very right and very normal. Come and take a trip with me through these pages. Let me offer answers to some of your questions, explain your emotions, and not only guide but also propel you through the next phases of your life.

For ten, fifteen, or even twenty years, you've studied, listened, and been tested in the academic world, but what about life's classroom? What about life's lessons? How many classes taught you about what you'll face every day and how to navigate your complex emotions and the baffling choices in front of you? You can have degrees, top honors, awards, accolades, and a promising career, but if you don't master everyday life strategies, you'll still be unhappy. You'll struggle unnecessarily. You can have a remarkable life ahead of you. If you write your own story, you also get to write the magnificent ending.

Envision an incredible four-hundred-year-old oak tree, its massive trunk with countless overreaching branches and thousands of dancing leaves. If you were to climb the tree, the strongest, most stable place to stay is near the trunk. If you climb out too far on the limbs, they'll bend and break.

Life is similar. One choice may take you onto a sturdy branch, but another may leave you dangling from a weak limb and wondering why. This book is designed to give you some directional cues to let you confidently navigate the tree of your life and feel confident as you climb. You may go off course instead of along a beautiful limb, but you'll have the guideposts to get you back on track.

What drives some people to have a positive attitude and excel throughout their lives while others struggle? Is it genetics? A secret green smoothie? An underground club few know about? Sure, genetics may play a small role, but for the most part, people who excel are those who accept themselves. They lean into life, and when they fall, they dust themselves off and get back into the game. They accept. They engage. They rise.

You've Got This! is a lifelong reference book to help you do just that. Join me on the journey of life as we explore these topics.

1. Starting Down the Path
How to harness the power of your mind.

2. Hitting a Bump in the Road
How to navigate life's struggles, such as setbacks, fear, pain, and addiction.

3. Traveling with Others

How to grow and manage relationships both in and out of the workplace.

4. Loving the Magnificent Journey

How to make wise choices so that you can embrace a joyful life.

This book was designed as a reference so that you can easily navigate to the area where you want to focus or need a little help. I encourage you to review it often, absorb the content, and take notes. Many times, we need to hear something multiple times for it to sink in. You are the author of your life. Give the pen to no one else.

Let's get started!

PART ONE

Starting Down the Path

CHAPTER 1

You Are Magnificent

Yes, you. *You* are magnificent. *You* are beautiful. You are an exceptional and resilient person who's consistently under construction.

Being "under construction" might sound discouraging; you may just want to jump to the finished product. However, we're never finished. Even your seventy-eight-year-old grandmother is learning something every day. We're all discovering how to navigate life and find our place in the world. That's the beauty of life. We're always growing and changing, and if we employ some key tactics, we're always getting better—always better.

You are special in your unique way. Be gentle with yourself and find the things to love about you.

Be yourself.

You have wonderful and unique traits that no one else can claim. The more time you spend being authentic, the stronger these distinctive traits become. You nurture and feed what makes you unique. You were born an original. Don't live as a duplicate. Anytime you act like someone else, you're cheating yourself out of potential and moving further away from the person you really are. It can be terrifying to be yourself, because what if people reject the true you? Isn't it better for them to reject a copy? That's a protection mechanism—*let me show the world an imitation so that I'm not vulnerable if they reject me.* That strategy may work to a point, but you'd be living a life that isn't yours. You'd never get to experience your true potential.

Be authentic and like-minded people will gravitate toward you. You're unique. Why should your path be any different?

What makes us unique? Are we just a handful of traits? No, we are not. What makes us unique are our activities. We are all working on various projects in our lives that many people know little or nothing about. You may decide to join a basketball league, volunteer at your local hospital, start reading an interesting book, or get back into snowboarding.

Ask people what they're excited about right now. What personal project are *you* working on? That which fills our time, mind, and soul is what makes us unique.

No individuals are the same or walking the same path every day and every minute. You are exceptional.

Nurture your magnificence and make your life extraordinary to match.

Give yourself permission to have the abundance and respect you deserve.

This, my dear, may be one of the most difficult concepts to grasp. Lean in, as this is probably what holds most people back in life. We often view our lives through our younger selves' eyes. "I don't deserve that big house, because I was only a C student." Or, "I want that job, but what do I possibly have to offer? Everyone in that company is probably so smart. I'm just a small kid from a small town. I'd never fit in."

Our life's abundance reflects what we believe we deserve. Think of something you strive to have—an authentic love, a dream job, a large house on a hillside, a travel budget. Now think of people you know who have one or all of those items. Why do they deserve them and you do not? You are just as worthy and deserving as they are. You need to give yourself permission for that abundance.

The world holds no limit on happiness. *Having abundance and a fulfilling life doesn't take away from anyone else.* Your joy should inspire others to strive for more. Don't shrink or give away your power. Stand tall and allow your abundant life to be their inspiration.

Be gentle with yourself. Love yourself.

We are usually our own toughest critics. How many times has a friend opened up to you about something upsetting he's done, but you feel he's being too hard on himself? Being kind to yourself should be at the top of your list. This opens and softens your heart.

Have you ever asked yourself, "Why am I living such a small life?" Perhaps because you have few loyal friends, you struggle with family and work. Perhaps you're just plain unhappy. You may feel this way due to the lack of confidence and love you have for yourself.

You are exceptional, and you have tremendous power. You can better love, nurture, and accept yourself in many ways.

1. Improve your own inner dialogue.
Speak to yourself the way you would speak to a friend. You would never call a friend names, but how many times have you called yourself names? You deserve better.

2. Avoid perfectionism.
No one is perfect. Never, I repeat never, be ashamed of who you are.

3. Support yourself, just as you would a friend. When you're nervous about a presentation, encourage yourself. Get excited and succeed!

4. Expand your world.
Try new things that interest you. Join a hiking group or soccer club. Attend a workshop on an intriguing subject. Take your dog to a dog-training program and meet new people. New stimuli will recalibrate your life, eventually

transforming you. The groups you join and people you meet are fortunate that you've entered their lives. Go out there and show them your magnificence.

> **YOU'VE GOT THIS:**
> You are marvelous. Love and nurture what's on the inside and everything else will fall into place.

CHAPTER 2

Harnessing the Power of Your Mind

O h, the mind is a mighty weapon! Do everything in your power to use it for your advantage and not against yourself.

You must protect your mind; it can be your most powerful tool or your weakest. The state of your mind affects your health, friendships, wealth, and happiness. The state of your mind radiates, pulling people in or repelling them.

The human mind is complex. Insecurity and loneliness can disrupt and morph reality, pulling you down when you are at your weakest. Yet while your thoughts define you, they also define who you're not. You can feed your thoughts with positive or negative energy. You can talk yourself into your dreams or out of them. So don't just make peace with your thoughts—employ them to move you toward your best life.

Everything has brought you to where you are today, even the challenges in your life. It may be difficult to understand, but your unique struggles build your unique strength. Like Legos or building blocks, your decisions, experiences, and genetics form who you are. Allow them to lift you up and make you more resilient, to make you ready to take on today. I couldn't believe it at the time, but looking back, I am grateful for every struggle and every mountain I had to climb. Each experience has provided a lesson and given me the strength to tackle the next chapter in my life.

When I was in my early thirties, I started a small company. It received some recognition, and the local NBC news station called me to ask for an interview. A dream come true? Wrong. I was driving when I received the call on my cellphone, but I had to pull over to a quiet parking lot. I was shaking and scared. *I'm just little Dina. I'm not worthy of an interview. What have I done? I'm a fraud, and now I'll be exposed.*

My business product was very valid, but I wasn't confident or ready to bring it to market. I didn't feel worthy of its possible success, so failure seemed more comfortable. The TV news interview went well, but I had a pit in my stomach. I was convinced I didn't deserve the attention.

Because I felt unworthy of success, my business never had a chance. I poured a lot of hours into that business, but rather than view it as a failure, I now deem it as one of the most valuable lessons of my life. Over time, I was able to look back and smile at my younger self and the insecure child she held inside. I was able to congratulate her effort. Now I know I wouldn't change a thing, not the time invested or the outcome.

What you think is how you feel. How many times do you read about people who defy the odds with their health, longevity, and limitations? It's the positive mind that propels us over the many hurdles we face. Your internal dialogue is a precursor to what will happen next. If you tell yourself you won't enjoy a party because you're not good at socializing, you likely won't.

The mind is powerful, but we often ignore it. We choose the right sneakers to cushion our feet with care, or we apply sunscreen to protect our skin, but what do we do to nurture our minds? Challenge yourself, keep a positive outlook, and keep going even when life gets tough. After all, it's not what you look at; it's what you see.

YOU'VE GOT THIS:
When faced with an opportunity, challenge, or decision, ask yourself, "What would I do if I felt 100 percent worthy?"

CHAPTER 3

Tapping into Mindfulness

Where are you right now? How does it smell? Is there a breeze skimming your cheeks? Is it daytime or nighttime? Are people around you? Redirecting your mind to the present moment is critical to happiness. If you're walking your dog, walk your dog. Be mindful of what you are doing and aware of everything around you. Let your senses draw in all of the stimuli. Notice the smells. Hear the birds chirping. Feel your dog's fur between your fingers as you stroke his head. Sense the warmth of the sun on your back. This is a form of meditation. It pulls us in and recalibrates our soul.

Because I was an avid multitasker, mindfulness was taxing for me. I thought I could cheat the system by doing three things at once. I had this down: I could walk the dog, check email on my phone, and socialize with the neighbors at the same time. What I began to realize, however, was that multitasking took a toll on me. I was twice as exhausted, so I wasn't getting ahead.

A few minutes of true mindfulness can recalibrate the soul and repair your day. One beautiful morning, I sat in the yard with our Great Dane. She was in the moment, watching the birds and dissecting the smells drifting her way. I took her cue and didn't think about work, emails, or the grocery list. Instead, I noticed her oddly shaped whiskers and watched the tip of her wet nose twitch. I recognized that the once-black fur around her eyes was turning into a gray mask.

Feel, see, and hear what's around you. Block out the ruminations that chatter in your mind. Be thankful for the moment and grateful you're experiencing it. Notice the butterflies, recognize the birds, and enjoy the leaves dancing in the wind.

The good news is that you can do this just about anywhere. When you commute to work or school, pay attention to the sunrise and the fresh air. When you're waiting for your plane to take off, notice other people and wonder about their life stories. Notice what you're doing and be aware of the beauty around you.

Practicing mindfulness gives our minds a rest. It pulls us out of our own heads and tunes us into the larger world. Mindfulness opens our hearts to what's unfolding right before us.

YOU'VE GOT THIS:
Practicing mindfulness nurtures the mind and soul just as nutrient-dense foods enrich the body.

CHAPTER 4

Staying in Your Lane

I t's difficult not to compare yourself with others. We often use comparison as a measuring stick to rate our own progress. We're raised from childhood to think this way. Games and tournaments have winners and losers. Classes have grades. (Conner got an A, but Jesse got a C.) However, if we compare ourselves to other people, we aren't identifying our own true ambitions; we're only trying to achieve what we *think* other people are achieving. That's not maximizing our personal potential.

1. Don't compare.
As I compose these pages, if I live to be ninety-six years old, I'm currently at my life's halfway point. I have never come across someone who "has it all." I'm not saying that to discourage you. I'm trying to illustrate that the outside

doesn't always reflect the inside. Someone might seem to have a great job, a wonderful spouse, a new house, a fancy car, and a killer game of basketball. What you might not see is that their spouse is struggling with mental illness or that they don't love their job, as they're only doing what's been expected of them since childhood.

You don't fully know someone else's history. Everyone has a different story built from his or her unique genes, childhood, experiences, and choices—it was crafted over a lifetime. Each situation is incredibly complex, but you are magnificent in your own unique way. *How could you possibly compare your path to another's?*

2. Don't compete with others.

We've all heard the phrase "keeping up with the Joneses." Consciously or unconsciously, we all try at some level to "keep up." This is unhealthy if it's only a matter of competition, but gauging your own performance against someone else's can also be positive. For instance, if someone is thriving, I want to know more about how that person is doing it. I'm inspired! At work, if a colleague submits a great report, I am motivated to leverage his or her ideas to better myself. I work harder the next time around. Conversely, if the same coworker sends out a poorly written report with little useful data, I never relish in their misstep. Their failure doesn't propel me.

Another example is within relationships. Often, people love to gossip by sharing negative information about someone else. This is a subconscious tactic people employ to push someone down in an effort to lift themselves up. Wish the best for everyone. *Other people's failures don't elevate you.*

YOU'VE GOT THIS:

No one can be *you* better than yourself— and you are pretty fantastic! If you try to be someone else, you will be only an imitation.

CHAPTER 5

Remaining Positive and Confident

onfidence is a big, juicy, important topic. Wouldn't you love to be confident all of the time? The truth is that *everyone* struggles with self-confidence. Yes, everyone, including the cocky NFL player, the gyrating rock musician, and the wealthy businessperson boarding a private jet. You see them in the spotlight in which they soar. What you don't see is that the NFL player faces an addiction problem, the musician struggles with a reading disorder, or the businessperson feels lonely and isolated.

No one is confident in every situation. We all have our strengths and weaknesses. Own and recognize your "weakness" as something to work on or accept. Don't spend your life fighting or hiding it.

In my experience, those who puff out their chests, swagger, and boast are usually the most insecure people in the room. They aren't convinced of their greatness, so they're trying to convince you of it.

Someone who is very academic may be strong in the classroom but inept at household tasks or fixing his car. Someone who has been told her whole life that she's beautiful may feel comfortable in social situations but shrink in other arenas. Someone who is naturally athletic may be in his prime at the gym but overshadowed in a face-to-face debate.

I know these are generalities, but often we see people when they shine and then assume they shine in every area. This depletes our own confidence. *No one shines or excels at everything.*

This became very clear to me at a dinner several years ago. Ten of us were gathered around a table. We had worked together for years, so we knew each other very well. I was known as someone who brings up "topics" to spur conversation. This had become a fun ritual for us. That night I asked everyone to think about what his or her greatest personal accomplishment was. Of what were they most proud?

The first person named her children. The next said that she was proud to be the first in her family to get a master's degree. So on and so forth, around the table it went, until we came to a coworker who we all knew was a great swimmer. He had won many awards, nearly qualifying for the Olympics. Of course, when it was his turn, he said that he was most proud of his accomplishments in swimming.

We then went around the table another time and I asked everyone to name a regret—nothing too dark or deep, just something light-hearted and funny. Someone answered that she regretted adopting her nutty, couch-chewing Labrador. Another person said that she regretted eating an entire pie the night before. When we got to the swimmer, he said that he regretted swimming.

The table fell silent. How much wine did he drink? Did he think we were still talking about our greatest accomplishments? I clarified that this question was about regrets, but he confirmed that his answer was swimming.

"Swimming is a solitary sport," he said. "I spent four to six hours a day in the pool with my head in the water while everyone else was socializing and building those skills. I struggle socially now."

I had known him for years and had no idea. Even this great swimmer, who was likely idolized on the starting blocks, setting new speed records and accepting awards—yes, even he struggled. No one has it all. No one excels in everything.

Scroll through your mind and picture some people who you are convinced have the self-confidence thing down. You're probably thinking, *They don't have any self-doubt! They walk into a room with their chest puffed out and head held high, their stride strong enough to push through a crowd.*

They are filled with confidence. They radiate it! Remember, though, that you don't know their whole story. You can't see the whole picture.

Everyone is insecure to various degrees and in different ways. Let's talk about what you can do about it.

1. Recognize when you feel insecure.

What are your triggers? This can be difficult because you have to be very honest with yourself. Your triggers have something to teach you. Write down a few things that you think might trigger insecurity within you. Don't hide from yourself.

2. React to the feeling.

Acknowledge the discomfort, but also learn to manage it. One helpful practice is to visualize tucking your insecurity into a far corner of your head. Now silently repeat, "I have no room for you in my head."

3. Decide how to respond.

Work on areas in need of improvement to master triggers that deplete your self-confidence. Or, simply decide to accept them, laugh them off, and move on. Make self-improvement a practice or simply live in your uniqueness. Don't let insecurity consume you.

4. Make simple physical changes.

- Posture: The simple act of pulling your shoulders back makes you look and feel more confident.

- Smiling: A smile will not only make you feel better but also make you more approachable. People will smile back, and the domino effect will begin.

- Eye contact: Look at the person to whom you are speaking, not at your shoes. Maintaining eye contact shows confidence to others and over time builds confidence in yourself.

Being confident and positive isn't always easy, but once you make it a practice and habit, it's life changing. We often don't know enough to make adequate judgments, so we should avoid negativity. Many times, we don't see the full picture when we're struggling. We don't see the end result until weeks, months, or years down the road. For instance, my son Ethan dislocated his ankle while playing tennis with his brother Owen. The bone broke through the skin and ended up needing surgery. He also contracted a staph infection that required a lot of attention, doctor appointments, and round-the-clock medications for six weeks.

Throughout this experience, Ethan did not complain. He chose to embrace the time we spent going to appointments and enjoyed our lunches afterward. He hobbled around school on crutches with a PICC line, but he never felt sorry for himself. He took responsibility for the energy he brought into a room and excitedly shared his well-earned scars and interesting story with others.

Laughing and crying may both give relief, but Ethan chose to laugh.

As a result of this experience, Ethan even developed a keen interest in the medical field. Had this injury not happened, he likely would never have been so intimately exposed to this career path. Through this accident, he might have found his calling.

As an animal lover, I've been told that many animals can sense our emotions. For instance, a dog you've never met will avoid you if you're insecure or fearful. When I took horseback riding lessons, the trainer explained that horses can sense nervousness. She advised me to take deep breaths to eliminate any pent-up anxiety in their presence. Both people and animals can sense the type of energy you bring into their space before you even say a word.

It is hard for almost everyone to grasp that you can go from nowhere to somewhere without even moving. In an instant, your state of mind can propel you or stop you; it can make you seem repellant or appealing. Make a decision to live in a beautiful state. Don't give up your happiness over little stuff or over what you can't control. Focus on what you *can* control and what you *can* do.

Being critical is easy, but what if we tried to be positive for just two weeks? Be playful and sincere. Be warm and inviting. Wear a smile. Studies show that even the act of smiling when you don't feel happy can lift your mood. People will gravitate toward you.

Those who are always complaining, blaming, or fearful are toxic to be around. When we practice gratitude, we appreciate life and radiate energy that pulls people toward us. Be grateful and focus on what you *do* have and everything will fall into place for you. If you focus primarily on what you *don't* have, you will forever struggle and never feel you have enough.

It's all in how you present it. You don't "have to" go to work: you "get to." After all, how many people are out there looking for a job right now? *The simple act of replacing "have" with "get" is life altering.*

YOU'VE GOT THIS:
No one is confident and positive 100 percent of the time. Small steps make mighty journeys.

CHAPTER 6

Unlocking the Magnificent You

I'll say it again. You are exceptional. You are magnificent. Now it's your turn to uncover who you *really* are and what you're passionate about.

If someone had asked me what I was passionate about a few years ago, my first answer would have been "I don't know." I'd never really scratched below the surface. I just went about my business, checking off my to-do list. I wanted to burn through my list and not dig deeper. In fact, I'd keep adding items to my list, mostly to avoid the question "who are you?" altogether. In reality, however, that should have been the first question on my list. Here are a few tips to guide you toward unlocking your magnificent self.

1. Get quiet, repair, and recalibrate.

First, bring yourself back to your center so that when you do the work, you're doing it with your true self. How many times are you influenced by different types of people and pulled off course? After a while, you might not feel authentic.

Spend some time alone. You cannot unlock who you are if you're being influenced externally. Bring your power back to be all that you are.

2. Discover what you are good at.

This too was hard for me, but through trial and error, I have realized that I'm extremely organized. At first, I assumed everyone else was like me, so I didn't think my organizational skills were exceptional. Eventually, friends began to notice my talent, even though I didn't. When they reached out to ask for organizing tips for their families, I realized that I had a special skill.

I know that being organized might sound a bit lame, but think of something that comes easily to you but is difficult for others. Identify anything, even something small. I work with someone who is a whiz with spreadsheets, operational data, and numbers, but for the life of him, he can't put his thoughts into a simple PowerPoint slide. Every time he has to present, he struggles. That's where I come in and use my organizational skills to add value. When you identify a few skills specific to you, write them down. Once you do, you can start finding ways to match them with a hobby or job.

3. Remember what you love to do and go do it!

A friend grew up playing soccer. He loved it, but now that he's in the workforce, he doesn't have as much time. Instead, he coaches a youth soccer team. I love dogs, so my rescue dog and I became a certified therapy team and now volunteer at our local hospital.

Get involved, but don't feel like it's a huge commitment. If it doesn't suit you, move on. Keep going. Keep testing the waters.

4. Expand your comfort zone.

Get out there and try new things, even the ones you're not entirely sold on doing. Join a club. Take a class. You will meet new people, learn something about yourself, and refine the list of what you enjoy.

5. Pay attention to your daydreams.

Go ahead. Write them down. You're the only one who will see your list.

6. Remember that you have the power to be, have, and do anything you desire.

Enough said.

7. Do not fear being "ordinary."

There is so much pressure to be extraordinary, but no one is extraordinary at everything. If the net sum of my strengths and weaknesses falls on an ordinary spectrum, I'm okay with that. I do know that I'm excellent at some things and not so fantastic at others. The key is to identify what you're good at, because that's what you usually enjoy.

8. Dabble a lot.

Once you have a list, you need to dabble a lot. Just as a honeybee goes from flower to flower, you should touch on many sources that might feed this list. The trick is to avoid a long commitment. For instance, when I first began volunteering with my dog, Tia, we went to a retirement community. I just didn't feel the connection, but I knew I did love visiting people with my dog. So, my next step was to try a different venue. We ended up going to our local hospital and have been there ever since.

Never feel ashamed of reallocating your focus. If you're not enjoying what you're doing, no one benefits. It's a win/lose.

YOU'VE GOT THIS:
Finding out who you are involves trial and error.
Have a sense of wonder about the world.
Dabble and be curious.

CHAPTER 7

When You Feel Frustrated, Angry, or Grumpy

These are tough emotions—hard to predict, difficult to control, and often challenging to remedy. Let's get through them together.

Darkness can surround you, but that doesn't mean it has to get inside of you. We all get angry, frustrated, and moody. The trick is to move through our feelings and resolve them sooner rather than later. The less time we spend in a dark place, the more time we spend in the light.

First, evaluate your feelings. Where do they fall on the spectrum? Are you fuming? Are you frustrated? Or, are you just in a grumpy mood? Each level has a slightly different antidote.

Second, now that you've identified your emotions, let's look at each one.

1. A bad mood

A bad mood can come from a variety and combination of triggers. Hunger, rejection, exhaustion, rumination, or disconnection—the list can go on and on. A few remedies are obvious. Eat or sleep if you're hungry or tired. Stay open and stand tall if you feel disconnected or rejected. If you think a friend blew you off, reach out again. If you haven't spent enough time to build your confidence, refocus. This is the time to push through those emotions.

Often, we can get out of a bad mood by hitting the pause button before we get too deep. Spend time in nature and realize the mood will pass. The first step is to know you're in a funk. The second is to identify its trigger and push against it. *Nothing you are upset about is unresolvable.*

2. Anger and frustration

The key here is facing your emotions. When you're livid and/or frustrated, nothing fans the flames more than feeling invalidated. What you need most at this time is to know that you deserve to have your feelings authenticated.

Consider a scenario where your refrigerator broke down, so you've had to live out of a cooler for weeks until the new one arrives. Anticipating its delivery, you take a day off from work and wait at the house. No one arrives, and when you call customer service, they tell you that your order isn't even going to ship for another few weeks.

How would you respond to the customer service agent if he said, "Why are you so angry? Your order will come in a few weeks." I don't think you'd feel any better. In fact, you'd be even angrier.

Now consider this response: "I hear you, and I can tell that you're very frustrated. I would be, too. It must have been difficult going weeks without a refrigerator and taking a day off from work. Here's what we're going to do for you. . . ." Whether you're the angry person or the one trying to cool that person off, emotional validation is the first best step toward resolving anger and frustration. We just want to be heard and authenticated.

Finally, remember that your life is good and you can make good choices. Don't give away your power to your emotions. Don't wait for things to get simpler or better. Life will always be complicated. Employ these methods to move forward in a positive way. After all, bad days are there to remind us to pay better attention to the good ones.

YOU'VE GOT THIS:

When you feel out of sync, hit pause and figure out a way to get back on track. Acknowledgement is the most difficult and critical first step.

CHAPTER 8

When Victimhood Creeps In

Life can be hard. At times, we may feel like the cards are stacked against us. You're allowed to feel this pain, but you're not to wallow or get stuck in the setback. We all have obstacles. It's how you deal with them that counts.

We can choose to walk in this world with a defeated heart or allow adversity to make us stronger. We all know people who blame, whine, or make excuses. Own what happens to you and don't complain. If you're struggling, set aside a small amount of time to feel the pain, but you must move on and decide not to stay in that state.

If you got a speeding ticket, the world isn't out to get you. Chances are that you were just going too fast. If you didn't get the job for which you interviewed, maybe you need to brush up on your skills; maybe they were looking for someone with more experience.

The decisions you make today are tomorrow's realities. Own your decisions. You are where you are because of your mindset and choices.

I remember sitting at lunch with a friend who I hadn't seen in a long time. He had struggled over the years with jobs, skipping from one to the next. Each time we'd talk, he'd complain about how bad the management was and how poorly he was treated. As we talked that afternoon, he told me he'd accepted a new position with a new company.

"How wonderful for you! Aren't you excited about new beginnings?" I asked.

He was stoic. "I guess. I'm not too hopeful this will be any better than the jobs I had before."

To me, that was the ultimate example of playing the victim. He had lost half a dozen jobs over ten years and every time, *they* were the bad guys. It was *their* fault he was unhappy. How could he possibly succeed when he saw himself as a victim even before his first day on the job? If he walked through those doors with a chip on his shoulder, he would get the same negative results he got on every other job. Greatness is earned; you get what you give. I suspect that even if he won the lottery he'd complain about being forced to decide where to deposit his winnings—checking or savings? He was sucking the life out of me.

Events, genes, and choices determine where you are in life. You may have been born into an abusive family, diagnosed with cancer, or hit by a car when you were walking on the sidewalk. Tragedies like this are beyond our control, but we have the power to choose how we react to them. Our choices make the difference in our lives.

We can be the passenger or sit in the driver's seat. In my life, I choose to drive, to be accountable and responsible. (Also, driving is more fun!) It's my responsibility to ensure I'm moving in the right direction. If something pulls me off course, it's up to me to get back in my lane. I will try not to complain, but rather be grateful for the experience. I'll search for what it taught me along the way so that I can do better the next time.

I try to imprint this on my three sons. My two oldest sons played tennis doubles for their high school team. During matches, I'd sit in the stands next to other parents. During one match, a parent was getting frustrated with the way her son was playing on a neighboring court. Apparently, he kept over hitting the ball, so it was going out. He and his doubles partner ended up losing the match.

When the match was over, the two boys came over to us on the bleachers. Her son's doubles partner asked him why he'd played poorly that day. A variety of excuses came up: the sun in his eyes, his new shoes, and his racquet that needed restringing. His partner pointed out that he too had the sun in his eyes. He too had new shoes. He too had not had his racquet restrung in quite some time.

Finally, her son said, "I don't know why! I just had a bad day, and then when I got frustrated, it just got worse!"

There, he peeled the layers off. He stopped playing the victim card. If he had said that in the beginning instead of making excuses, it would have been so much more authentic and it would have given him the knowledge to adjust his mindset. When he continued to blame the sun, his shoes and his racquet, he was incapable of getting past his own victimhood because those were just excuses. Often, when we start to struggle, it's very difficult to get back on track, especially when we mislabel our challenge. No one is always at the top of his game.

You don't need excuses. Show up and get the job done. If you're struggling, be honest and authentic. Don't use the victim card, whine, or complain. If you're reading this book, life is pretty good for you.

We do not always perform at the top of our game; that's the time to identify the truthful reason why. Maybe that tennis player was just "off" that day; maybe a few bad shots killed his confidence. It happens. Don't place blame where it doesn't belong. You can't solve the issue when you can't name the trigger. Identify it. Own it. Learn from it.

YOU'VE GOT THIS:

It's all about perspective. Life can happen *to* us or *for* us. "It's a poor craftsman who blames his tools."

CHAPTER 9

How to Ignore the Noise in Your Head

Oh, that little elf in your head who just keeps talking—he can build you up or cut you down. Why would you ever choose the latter? The truth is that *you* are the one who decides what the elf says.

How many times do you relive a moment that you feel wasn't your best? For instance, we may not fully listen to someone, and therefore our response is off. At the coffee shop, the barista says, "Isn't it a nice day today?"

You respond, "I'm good, thanks."

Afterward, you're embarrassed. You can't stop thinking about it.

Or, you visit with a friend. Later you go over the conversation and overanalyze your responses. Did you say the wrong thing?

Maybe you play touch football with some buddies and get hammered on the field. After that, you hate running into them; it constantly bugs you that they saw you at your worst.

This is called *ruminating*. It's the nasty loop that goes around and around in our head as we question our experiences, insecurities, or frustrations. To combat it, you'll need to identify what's effective and what's not.

With the barista, just laugh it off or vow to be more present, to listen before responding. With friends, make a decision to correct yourself if you feel you misstate something, rather than letting it go. After too much time, it can be awkward to bring up again. If you didn't perform at your best or embarrassed yourself, either learn from it or let it go, but don't relive it over and over. Honestly, 95 percent of the time, you remember the situation when no one else does. You blow it out of proportion through the unproductive and destructive loop in your head. After a while, that loop morphs reality.

Be aware. When you find yourself ruminating (for me it's during any quiet moment, like hiking, driving, or folding laundry), acknowledge that you're stuck in a negative loop and redirect your mind to a pleasant thought. It's quite effective: soon, the loop stops. We're often too hard on ourselves, analyzing and reliving our mistakes when everyone else has moved on.

Also, recognize that we can be our own toughest critics. To ourselves, we say awful things that we would never say to anyone else:

"I'm not funny or quick witted; people probably think I'm boring."

"I'm stupid. I just don't get the concepts as quickly as John does."

"I'm fat and out of shape."

First, you are handsome, beautiful, smart, and exceptional! Second, thoughts are like seeds. If you plant negative thoughts, they will dig their roots deep into your mind and soul, grab hold of you, and pull you down. If you plant positive ones, a beautiful seedling will emerge, leaning toward the sunlight as it climbs to the sky.

> **YOU'VE GOT THIS:**
> Make an effort to acknowledge the chatter—
> that elf—in your mind; replace the negative
> words with the positive.

CHAPTER 10

Accepting a Compliment

It's difficult for many of us to accept a compliment. You may feel embarrassed or unworthy of the praise, or maybe you're trying to be humble. However, when you argue against a compliment, in a sense you are challenging the person who is giving it to you.

Until recently, accepting a compliment was hard for me. A dear friend and I went to a painting class. In that class, we were instructed to paint aspen trees in a forest. I already had a few of those types of nature paintings around the house, so I decided to do something different from the rest of the class. Instead, I painted a picture of tulips. When the instructor said time was up, I stepped back, pleased with my version of the flowers.

My friend looked over my shoulder. "Wow, that's beautiful!" she said.

Embarrassed, I shrugged it off. "Oh, I don't know. It's not that good." I wanted to be humble, and the compliment had made me uncomfortable.

"Well, I think it's great," she said. "So just say thank you."

She was right. I was proud of my painting, but I didn't have the courage to own the fact that I had created something beautiful. Since that experience, I have decided simply to say thank you to a compliment. I have vowed to own it.

YOU'VE GOT THIS:

When you receive a compliment, accept it and simply say thank you. (A little smile and some eye contact helps, too.)

CHAPTER 11

Taking Good Care of You

The best thing you can do is take care of your exceptional mind and mighty body.

We've all heard the phrase "You are what you eat," but I'd never thought about it much until recently. To me, eating was a social activity, a daily routine that I looked forward to, but not because I was nourishing my body. Food tasted good and meals were something to do. A dinner and a movie seemed no different from each other. Both were fun and entertaining.

Over the course of a year, I began incorporating healthier foods into my diet: green smoothies, more vegetables and fruits, and various teas. Before long, this became a habit. Soon, I began to crave these nutritionally dense foods over most processed foods. As though that wasn't surprising enough, people began to compliment me on my skin. I looked healthier; I had more energy. My body was responding in thanks. Don't get me wrong. I still love cheese curls and fried food, but where once they were my staple, now they are my splurge.

Our bodies are miraculous. If you take care of your body, it will do its best to take care of you. Over the past few years, we've been increasingly bombarded with drug advertisements: "If you have an ache, ask your doctor about this new drug." The other night, I counted six drug commercials within an hour-long program. It's as though we're being taught to skip healthy eating and exercise and run for a pill to erase our bad choices. I'm not implying medicines aren't necessary. I'm simply stating that turning to medication as a first choice is becoming more acceptable.

In my view, no magic pill exists. One spring, about ten years ago, my nose was running. I thought it was hay fever, so I took an over-the-counter allergy pill for a few months. It seemed to make me thirsty, so I switched brands. A few months after that, my nose seemed irritated. Someone suggested I take nasal sprays to help. Then I began to get headaches and fatigue, so on the advice of my doctor, I incorporated sinus washes and a humidifier in my bedroom.

After a few years and half a dozen new nasal sprays (over-the-counter and prescription), I thought I was a lost cause. At this point, I was taking two different allergy pills, two nasal sprays, and a nasal gel to get rid of the dryness the sprays had caused. I was also doing twice-daily sinus washes and sleeping with the humidifier.

One day, I decided to stop it all. I was terrified; after all, I thought I was an allergic mess. Within a week, my headaches, fatigue, runny nose, and sneezing were all gone. I felt terrific. I'm now convinced that what prompted this avalanche of medication was a very mild cold. Instead of letting Mother Nature take her course, I started an unnecessary, commercially prompted, pill-popping, nose-spraying cycle. I should have left Mother Nature alone.

I believe health is contagious. We think of illness or disease as contagious, but so is well being. It is said that if you share news of any kind, it has four degrees of separation. In other words, it affects four more people down the line. So if you've found a great, new, healthy habit, share it with others. If you lose ten pounds, share your accomplishment!

I'm not implying that medications aren't useful; they can save lives and make living more comfortable. I do think we need to ask ourselves if altering our lifestyle instead could bring a better resolution to our ailment. When properly cared for, living beings of all kinds are incredible little machines. Mother Nature alone will often reward you with life's greatest assets: health and comfort.

YOU'VE GOT THIS:

Take care of your body as naturally as possible—
as Mother Nature intended—and it will likely
take care of you.

PART TWO

Hitting a Bump
in the Road

CHAPTER 12

When a Setback or Failure Happens

Failures or setbacks happen to everyone, but that doesn't make them any easier. I'm here with you—like everyone in the world, I have experienced failure. It's impossible to live without failing at something. If you live that cautiously, your life is a failure by default. Luckily, setbacks have many benefits. No matter how long the dark tunnel, there is light at the end.

You may have many mistakes and failures in your past, but be true to yourself. Acknowledge that you *were* that person, but you no longer *are*. As hard as it may seem, see setbacks as small gifts. When you live through them, you become secure in your ability to survive.

Consider this—failure helps you to correct your course. If your path doesn't feel right, turn back—*no matter how far you've traveled*. Your gut is usually right. Tune into it. It can save you time and pain.

Everyone who has ever accomplished something big, or even something mildly significant, has experienced a setback. It's just that you haven't heard about their failures.

When you're watching a movie, you don't realize the star on the screen went to 300 auditions and failed 299 times. All you see is the one success. When you see a star athlete on the field or court, you don't see the hundreds of thousands of athletes who never made it to that level.

Every time you allow a setback to affect you negatively, you're giving your power away. Look at failure as a chance to learn how *not* to do something. When we have a bad experience, we hold onto, rehearse, and relive it. We need to let it go. A setback can do a number on our confidence. It can distort our self-perception and make us question ourselves: "Why did I try that? What was I thinking?"

Failure also distorts our idea of the goal itself. If we fail at something, we often place a higher value on that experience. We start to prize what we think we can't have. Finally, failure plays a trick on our minds and makes us think success is beyond our control. These mind games are a toxic and destructive combination.

When you have a setback, you need to get moving. Don't stop your life for recovery—move to discovery. The trick is to regain control in small steps. Improve your self-talk and create a plan. If you were laid off, take time to nurture your soul, but now is not the time to play the victim. Get your fight on and move forward one step at a time. Consider what you've learned; move on to where you'd like to work next. Get busy. *Confidence after a setback comes from progress.* The more you sit, the more you wither away.

The bottom line is, there are ways to take control of any situation, even when it seems impossible. We have to conquer our defeatism. Move forward one small step at a time and take back control of your life. Sometimes you need to write a bigger story for yourself. Like a plant, don't remain in the same small pot—give yourself the room to grow!

YOU'VE GOT THIS:

Failing is winning. Don't worry about your failures; worry about the opportunities you will miss if you dwell on them.

CHAPTER 13

Facing Those Hard-to-Get-out-of-Bed Mornings

Yawn. I know—nothing feels better than staying under those warm covers in the morning. Nevertheless, often you can't, and you shouldn't. So how do you make it easier?

The mind is miraculous, so use it to your advantage. When you want nothing more than to pull the sheets up over your head, try a simple but effective trick. In your mind, repeat three times, "It's going to be a great day."

With the first iteration, you won't believe what you're telling yourself; it will seem silly. By the third time, however, something will click. A small part of you will begin to believe it. Sometimes that's all it takes—a little belief that today is a blessing.

Go ahead. Give it a try. I won't tell anyone.
What I think is how I feel.

> **YOU'VE GOT THIS:**
> Extraordinary thoughts are the beginning
> of an extraordinary day.

CHAPTER 14

Learning from Mistakes

I've never told this story, but my cursor sits blinking on the screen as if it's asking me to tell it. You win, little cursor. You win. I would be a hypocrite if I didn't bring this example to light. When I thought about what we learn from our mistakes, this story came to me first.

I've worked at a very large company for over twenty years. The teams I work with have become almost like family. We talk every weekday, travel together, and know each other well. Every year, we attend a weeklong event with over a thousand team members from around the world. We socialize, brainstorm, and connect. It's a true working forum.

However, the work environment for me has always been a delicate dance between knowing your coworkers personally while keeping it professional. The longer you work with people, the more difficult this dance. One night during our annual event, we were at a restaurant and bar. I was talking with one of our top sales reps who lived on the East Coast. She had a mixed drink and then elbowed me to join her for a second, which turned into a third. My head was spinning, my judgment skewed and my personality temporarily altered by the alcohol.

As the evening went on, I mustered up the confidence to walk over and strike up a conversation with our vice president, with whom I rarely spoke. The evening came to an end, so we boarded the bus and were driven back to the hotel.

The next morning I woke up mortified. *What had I done? What were the company and employees saying about me? I've ruined my personal brand. I'm such an idiot!*

I could either hide or fight. After a week of torture and ruminating, my fight came out. I decided I needed to release this burden I was carrying around. I had to face it. I had to find the gain in my pain. The only way out was to call and apologize to the vice president. Knowing I might forget everything because of nerves, I wrote down a few carefully crafted sentences. I dialed his number, and on the first ring, he answered! With shaking, sweaty hands, I read my sentences aloud. When I was done, I closed my eyes, waiting to be chastised or blown off.

The opposite happened. He told me that I was brave and that not a lot of people would have had the courage to make that call. I apologized again and we ended our

I will never forget when my husband and I bought our dream home in 2008. We were in awe of it. We couldn't believe it was ours. When I looked at the large stone pillars in the front, the pond filled with lily pads in the back, and the massive staircase, I felt as if I needed to pinch myself.

One day soon after moving in, my mom and I were in the front yard with the dogs when a neighbor walked by. She came into our yard to introduce herself. My mom beamed at her.

"Hi, I'm Margie, Dina's mom. I am so proud of her and Bob." She waved her arm toward the house. "They did this all themselves. We didn't help them one bit."

I didn't understand why she went out of her way to say that. I was a little embarrassed. In time, though, I realized that she was proud. She was proud because it's a beautiful home, but, more important, she knows that material things don't bring joy. What counted was the achievement—that we did it ourselves.

Society skews the meaning of true success. Be gentle with yourself and careful not to rate your achievements based on your paycheck. Money can make you powerful or powerless. Your spending habits reflect what you value. Money can't deliver friendship, love, companionship, or a sense of accomplishment. It should provide for you, but if it becomes the center of your life, it could cost you your happiness.

YOU'VE GOT THIS:

Money can buy luxuries, but not the most important ones. Money can ease burdens, but not all of them.

CHAPTER 16

What about What Others Think?

Let's start with the fact that I think—I know—you're pretty spectacular. When you live your life based on what other people think, you consciously or unconsciously make choices to meet their standards, not yours. Don't give your power away.

A former neighbor of mine used to invest so much time putting on the pretense of a perfect life, of optimum health and wealth. She was so worried about what other people thought of her that she alienated her family and exhausted herself. She was constantly pretending. What she didn't realize is that people could sense her inauthenticity, which pushed them away.

Here are some tips to help you live your own authentic life.

1. Remember that people are wrapped up in their own world.

They aren't thinking what you believe them to be. Be kind and people will think highly of you. Don't try to fool them with a counterfeit life.

2. Remember the 20-50-70 rule.

At age twenty, we tend to worry about what people think of us. At age fifty, we realize people aren't thinking about us as much as we thought they were. By the time we're seventy, we really don't care what, if anything, people think of us.

3. Remember to recognize insecurity.

Acknowledge and identify when insecurity arises, but always push it aside. Often, your childhood creeps in—the time when you were embarrassed at school, your crush broke your heart, or the soccer team rejected you. When childhood insecurities happen, create a small corner in your mind and say to yourself, "I have no space for you."

YOU'VE GOT THIS:
Make good choices. Your own conscience and high standards dwarf the opinions of others.

CHAPTER 17

When the Pain Gets Real

Pain—I wish I could make it go away, but I can't. Only you can. We want to escape from uncomfortable, icky feelings as soon as possible. Yet, sometimes there is no quick fix.

So how do we deal with pain? Let's go through a few options.

First, we need to recognize what we're feeling. This may seem easy, but like ostriches, we want to stick our heads in the sand. Ignoring pain, however, doesn't make it go away. In fact, if you ignore the pain, it can manifest in other areas, growing and festering. A small problem can become larger, branching out like roots of a tree. Soon, the intertwined mess underneath the surface is more difficult to unravel.

Second, understand that self-soothing and numbing can come in a variety of disguises. Consider that your actions may be tied to pain. Anything you do to avoid what you're feeling is called *numbing*. Do you have an occasional drink or do you down several vodka tonics? Do you savor every bite of the cupcake or gulp down half a dozen without even noticing the flavor? Do you constantly stay busy, rush around, and focus on minutiae because you're afraid of what you'll face if you take a little downtime?

What about social media? What are you avoiding when you're behind the computer screen? Beware of shiny objects that pull you in, these easy, seductive distractions from pain. And remember, pain can be as simple as boredom. These are the moments we need to get to work, not to drink, surf the web, flip channels, or otherwise numb ourselves.

Third, don't try to escape the pain by creating a new problem in its place. This is also a form of avoidance and distraction. Several years ago, a friend of mine lost her job. Rather than reenter the workforce, she decided to stay at home and focus on raising her two daughters for a few years. However, she kept telling me that she longed for more. Naturally, as her children grew, they spent more time with their friends and in various activities.

This took a toll on my friend. She felt bored and unneeded. Over time, she began to develop small health symptoms: an upset stomach, allergies, headaches, and fatigue. This went on for years. I reached out, but she withdrew from her friends and spent more time alone.

One day, she called and invited me for coffee. She looked terrific and had a lot of energy. She told me that she had recently begun volunteering and that the organization had offered her a full-time position. She explained that even though she had been miserable home alone on the couch, it had become easier than facing the truth: that the company to which she had dedicated many years had rejected her and that her growing children now needed her less than ever. She had realized that her illness had become the lesser of two evils, a distraction for what she was feeling. It was a self-induced protective mechanism.

I'm certainly not implying that illnesses don't exist or are always self-induced. What I am saying is that in her hopelessness my friend created a distraction to avoid facing her agony. When she shared this with me, her openness brought me to my knees. I loved her honesty and vulnerability.

Finally, lean into the pain. You have to go through the darkness to get to the light. It's hard, but it's the only way out. Label what you're feeling and figure out its source. Come up with a plan to get through it. Numbing and avoidance will only lead to more challenges and become a slippery slope. Before you realize it, a failed relationship will turn you into an Internet addict who's lost his job, his once sky-high confidence hovering at ground level. This is the time to do your work. Lean into the truth; find a solution and pull yourself out of the pain one day, one step at a time.

YOU'VE GOT THIS:
When you're doing something you know isn't good for your body and soul, investigate the "why."

CHAPTER 18

What about the "Addiction Gene"?

I know of little else that has torn families apart, destroyed lives, or shattered dreams more often than addiction. Alcohol, drugs, smoking, gambling, food, video games, shopping—the list goes on and on. I've watched wonderful people drift away under the spell of addiction, the same people who love their family and children with wide arms and open hearts. If sober, these same people would be mortified to watch themselves choose their addiction over anything—anything— else.

Some researchers say there is an "addiction gene," a virtually invisible lever that we unconsciously pull inside of us. This invisible lever is powerful. Worse, it often goes undetected until your life begins to unravel.

No magic answer to addiction exists, so tune into your behaviors and mental state as often as you can. Place your actions in two groups: "radar" and "hell no!"

The "radar" category includes things that you might do regularly, but if taken too far could become addictive behaviors—you need to keep them on your "radar." These might include shopping, video games and technology, food, alcohol, gambling, and so forth. If you become sucked into these behaviors, identify them early, be honest with yourself, and dig deeper to find out why. Why did you overeat again and gain ten pounds this year? Why did you *really* pour that gin and tonic while sitting alone? Why are you doing anything to excess? Are you numbing pain? Are you running from something?

By identifying the cause that drove you to these behaviors, you can then begin to fix them, rather than to numb or avoid. The key here is to check in and check in often. You have to stay on top of any yearnings that become excessive behaviors.

The "hell no!" category is a bit more cut and dry. These are non-negotiable, stay-away-from-me activities, including drugs of any kind, anything illegal, and smoking. You could argue that alcohol could fall here, but I place it in the "radar" category.

Individuals have to decide for themselves where they feel most comfortable. However, I've seen people take a seemingly harmless puff from a cigarette and be hooked the following week. I have a neighbor whose son is battling lung cancer in his late twenties. If you're looking for cigarettes or drugs, deeper emotions need to be resolved. Substance abuse isn't a resolution to anything.

You are in control. Check in with yourself often, scan your behavior, and be brutally honest about your yearnings. Life can crumble in a moment through a few bad choices. Why add complexity to life when you're only trying to find your way?

Choose to pull the lever on an exceptional life instead!

YOU'VE GOT THIS:
Addiction—beware and be aware.

CHAPTER 19

When People Are Mean

Can't we all just get along and live in a fairy-dusted world with unicorns and rainbows? Unfortunately, that's not the case. It stinks when people are mean, but we can try to understand the source of their behavior. We can even reduce or eliminate its effect on us and ensure we don't deposit any more meanness into the world.

One definition of mean is "small." The way people treat you is a reflection of who they are. It has nothing, nada, zilch to do with you. However, you cannot forgive what you do not understand. In order to get past it, look at the root cause.

Think of a time when you were irritated or having a bad day. Maybe you were really hungry and the waiter made a mistake on your order. Maybe you bumped into a friend who just aced a test that you failed. How did you react to these additional frustrations? When people lash out, they are mirroring their own unhappiness and dissatisfaction. Their behavior is a window into their heart, a glimpse of what their soul is feeling at that moment.

When someone hurts someone else, it's all about what you didn't see. You didn't see the envy in their eyes when they looked at you. You didn't see them struggle that morning with their mentally disabled sibling. You didn't see them fight to get out of bed because they're struggling with a recent rejection or an abusive past.

Now think of a time when you were on top of the world. You just got great news and felt that everything was wonderful. You entered the restaurant hungry and the waiter made a mistake on your order. What was your reaction? How did it differ from the time when you were frustrated? What if you bumped into a friend who aced his test? Would you give him a high five or a cut down?

Here is a subtle example of cruelty that we see in different forms. One summer, I bumped into a very fortunate friend. She has a home in our neighborhood, a condominium in the beautiful Rocky Mountains, and another home on a lake in Idaho. Knowing that she recently spent several weeks in her Idaho home, I asked her about it. After she told me tales of driving the boat on the lake and paddleboarding, I asked if she had another adventure planned for her family before the summer was over. She wrinkled her nose and hesitantly said that they were going to their condo for a few weeks.

"Good for you!" I replied.

She gave me a huge, surprised smile. "Thank you!" she said. "You know, a lot of people give me a hard time about spending so much of our summer in Idaho or the mountains. It's refreshing to hear support."

At the time, my friend couldn't understand the basis for everyone else's reactions. To me, they were either envious or missed her when she was away. Regardless, my friend should have taken their responses as compliments.

I'm not implying that we should tolerate another person's nastiness. First, though, realize its source. Most of the time, small, stern comments are not worth addressing. Second, never add to the negativity. Don't create a continual toxic loop, a merry-go-round that will be hard to get off. Stop the momentum. Third, if a particular cruelty warrants addressing, first ask for clarity. In other words, ask them to repeat their negative remark: "What do you mean?" A question like this often makes people realize their misstep and gives you time to think on your toes. It doesn't imply that they get a free pass, but it demonstrates that you don't take their meanness personally.

Never make someone else's cruelty about you. They have their own struggles, their own stories, and their own dissatisfactions. They are projecting them onto you, although doing so is counterintuitive; it doesn't make their own pain go away. When people hurt you, you can only expect them to give at the level of which they are capable at that moment. We make a mistake if we expect people to give at our own level if they have only half our capacity.

> **YOU'VE GOT THIS:**
> You can't be happy and mean at the same time.

CHAPTER 20

Four Steps to Overcome Rejection

Rejection hurts. You offer yourself to a person, a job, or a situation, but they deny or refuse you. *Ouch.* The important thing to realize is that everyone—yes, everyone—has felt rejection.

As much as I've always wanted to protect the ones I love, to wrap my arms around them and shield them from the world, to do so long-term would be damaging. We've all been rejected, but only a few brave people muster up the strength to ever think about it, much less share the embarrassment with anyone else.

In reality, talking about rejection is one of the bravest things someone can do. You can't talk about it to just anyone, however. The person you talk to has to be "safe," someone who will honor you and cradle your spirit in his hands with as much care as he would his own.

When you feel hurt and rejected, here are four steps you can take.

1. Don't give away your power.
The more you allow rejection to upset you and alter your path, the more power you are feeding it. You tried for something. You will try again tomorrow, maybe with a new focus or maybe not.

2. Know your chances for success.
If you know early on that what you're trying to gain is a long shot, the rejection may not be as devastating.

3. Keep several irons in the fire.
If you sent in applications to seven companies and the first one didn't come through, you'll feel more hopeful with six more on the horizon. You will also feel proud of yourself for making a big effort, not just a minimal one.

4. Realize that rejection is usually not a reflection of you.
The company you applied for may have had needed a candidate who was located in a specific region. The girl who broke your heart may have deeper, personal challenges that she hasn't shared with anyone and needs to sort out for herself. Behind the decision-making process is a bigger and broader reality than you know. You may not understand this until much time has passed, but whatever *does* eventually work out for you is usually a better fit than what initially rejected you.

YOU'VE GOT THIS:

Rejection is a part of life. As painful as it feels at the time, rejection builds resilience and strength, so you can cope better the next time around. Bonus—it probably wasn't meant to be in the first place.

CHAPTER 21

Regaining Perspective

I f that's your biggest problem, you've got it pretty good." That's what my mother would tell me anytime, and I mean *anytime*, I complained. Now I lovingly say the same thing to my sons. I'm not implying that life isn't sometimes tough or that you will never feel defeated. I am saying that you should be careful to apply to any problem *only* the relative level of energy it requires. This wisdom has served me well, and my hope is that it will do the same for you.

Our biggest addiction is not to drugs, cigarettes, or alcohol. Our biggest addiction is to creating problems in our lives that really don't exist. We tend to be fearful— fearful of success, of happiness, or of not being enough. We suffer in a state of "loss," "never," and "less." This is really an obsession with ourselves. When we practice perspective and gratitude, we change the course of our habitual, negative way of thinking.

Blowing things out of proportion can easily become a cycle. Because our mind is complex, many factors may cause us to do this. We may be bored or unfulfilled. On occasion, making a small issue into a larger one feels more familiar than accepting the sensation of boredom.

Sometimes, we may even feel more joy than we're comfortable with. We may sabotage our happiness by blowing an issue out of proportion. We may want to decrease our level of joy because it's beyond what we allow ourselves to accept. When we're sabotaging our joy, we're sabotaging ourselves.

Finally, we may simply get so focused on our own world that we don't see beyond the challenge. We don't recognize that it's being served to us on a silver platter. Instead, we think about it. We ruminate about it. Soon, we've given the problem more attention than it deserves.

This happened to me not too long ago. I had a new boss whom I found very challenging to work with. As much as I tried, I just couldn't grasp what he wanted and needed. Our collaboration wasn't on target. Soon, I was feeling defeated and exhausted.

One day, I had a meeting with my new boss and was assigned a to-do list longer than an Olympic-sized swimming pool. To soothe myself, I went into the hospital with my therapy dog. As I mentioned earlier, I volunteer with my dog Tia at our local hospital, visiting staff and patients to brighten their day. This day, I visited the surgery waiting area, where friends and family stay while their loved ones are in surgery. A dear neighbor of mine was waiting there. I approached her and asked if everything was okay. She said her son was just diagnosed with lung cancer. A team of doctors was performing tests and deciding on a course of action. She looked exhausted, heartbroken, and defeated.

I entered the hospital that day feeling a little sorry for myself, as though my challenge was greater than anyone else's. After seeing my neighbor, though, my difficulties seemed very small and manageable. In fact, I drove home from the hospital with a sense of gratitude for my job and for the personal challenge it afforded me. If that was my biggest problem, I had it pretty good.

Yes indeed, I do have it *really* good.

YOU'VE GOT THIS:
"If that's my biggest problem, I've got it pretty good."
Yes. Yes you do.

PART THREE

Traveling with Others

CHAPTER 22

Why Kindness Matters

When you make someone shine, you shine too. Some people in this world are just plain kind. You gravitate toward them; you feel a sense of softness and peace. When you're with them, you know you won't be belittled, mocked, or judged.

When I walk into a school, volunteer situation, work function, or crowded room, I naturally move toward someone I know will be "safe" to approach. When I say "safe," I don't mean physically; I mean emotionally. This person won't hurt my feelings, pick on me, or lash out if they're having a bad day. My emotions are safe in their presence.

We all know unpredictable people. One day, they're all smiles and hugs. The next day, they cut you down to your core. Your experience with them is a rollercoaster, a gamble every time.

Of course, we all have bad days. We can certainly share our struggles, but we should never lash out and create pain for others. *Their pain doesn't eliminate our own.*

Sometimes, one can be unconsciously harsh and unknowingly hurt someone's feelings. Name one thing at which you excel. Do you ever make other people who don't excel at that same thing feel inadequate? Think of a time when someone shared a moment with you when she felt that she wasn't at her best: she didn't do well on a test, in an interview, or on the sports court. Did you support her or add to the injury? Be aware of how your actions are received by others.

Be encouraging and uplifting, as well. Kindness can be subtle. When you're shopping, smile and make eye contact with those who are helping you. If you see an elderly person, acknowledge them with a smile.

Let's take on the challenge of being "safe" for others. We can be the type of person who people trust with their emotions. We will not cut them off at the knees to serve our own purposes. It doesn't matter where we are in life— in school, at the office, or at play—we can operate in the "safe zone" for others. When we make others shine, it reflects back upon us.

YOU'VE GOT THIS:
Being kind toward another rewards you twice over.

CHAPTER 23

Family
A Deep and Sometimes Complicated Love

Family falls anywhere on the spectrum of our greatest joy to our deepest pain. We laugh together and cry together. We've seen each other at our best and at our worst. We are born together and grow old together.

Win/win scenarios make family relationships healthy and long lasting. Both parties need to benefit from the connection. That's when a beautiful bond is created. For example, I do not want my three sons to be with me because they feel obligated. I want them to be with me because they truly want to spend time in my presence. This makes me strive to be a better person, too.

Is a win/win scenario realistic with every family member? Probably not. I don't know of any family where *every* member has a win/win connection with each other.

If a parent, grandparent, or sibling is demanding, abusive, or just plain hard to be around, the other family members will likely drift away.

No one should continually sacrifice his or her life and time for a win/lose scenario. Sometimes when you're expected to attend a family gathering, you may do so grudgingly. A situation like this should be weighed very carefully. Is the loss on your end greater than the gain? Will someone make you feel guilty if you don't attend? If so, is it worth fighting against? The disruption might be difficult short-term but worth it for the long-term gain.

The deep-rooted relationships between family members can get complicated. We often don't hold our family to the same standards as we would others. However, I believe family members do need to be held accountable. Being your family doesn't give them the right to disrespect, abuse, or exploit you. Every healthy relationship is earned. Be true to yourself and set boundaries. Have standards for everyone—yes, even family.

If necessary, rewrite your family dynamics. Sometimes people say, "But he's my brother," or "She's my mom." They don't get a free pass, period. We are not required to do for them blindly because they are family.

A good example of this is what my dear friend Debbie has experienced. Debbie's older brother Phil lives with their mother. Phil moved in with her two years ago because he is unemployed and could no longer pay his bills. He has no family of his own, and he has alienated many friends.

Debbie contributes financially to support Phil, who now relies entirely on Debbie and their mother. He says he's looking for a job but shows no evidence of this. Debbie isn't wealthy, but she works hard and does what she can to help Phil. However, he is not helpful around the house. He complains and shows no gratitude.

When Debbie recently made the six-hour drive to see Phil and her mother, she went grocery shopping so that she could prepare dinner for the three of them. Phil wanted to come along. In the car, he yelled at her, saying she was spoiled and calling her a host of disrespectful names.

After all she has done for her brother, Debbie was confused and angry. She called me when they returned from the store; she was a wreck. I suggested that she stand up for herself, but she was hesitant because "he's family." He intimidated her. As a little girl, she looked to him as a father figure, so how could she possibly defy him?

Unfortunately, that visit was not much different from any other. When Debbie returned home, she was exhausted. She was clear that she was only putting up with Phil because he is her brother. To me, Debbie could take this opportunity to set boundaries. She could say, "I will not speak to you unless you can be calm and respectful. I will also no longer support you. You are a very capable person who can get a job and be independent. When you are willing to have a healthy, respectful relationship with me, I'm here, but until then, I wish you the best."

Other damaging and hard-to-spot tactics are manipulation and guilt. Sometimes family expectations are beyond what you're willing to give, but family will manipulate and guilt you into doing something. Keep guard of the company you keep and set boundaries for everyone in your life—family included.

It's like the old story goes: if you squeeze a bird too tightly, when you open your hand, it will likely fly away. If you always hold your hand open in a kind, accepting way, the bird will be more likely to return on its own. Relationships are the same. Mutual respect is the foundation of *every* connection.

YOU'VE GOT THIS:
Every relationship, including family, should be mutual and respectful.

CHAPTER 24

Noting What You're Doing and Who You're With

If you let your authentic self shine, anyone and everyone is fortunate to be in your company.

When it came to whom I kept as company, my dad used to tell me, "Water seeks its own level." If I didn't feel good about myself, I would likely surround myself with like-minded others. Just like water, they would be at my level—low and shallow. Equally, people who were positive would have less interest in being with me if I brought them down. Instead, they would seek people at their own, higher level.

Time is precious. If you surround yourself with people who don't support you, then like an anchor off a boat, they will hold you stagnant, or worse, drag you down. Choose your friends wisely. It is said that you are the sum total of the five people you spend the most time with. Stand guard of your heart and mind. Protect your magnificent spirit and soul from negative influences.

You cannot sacrifice your potential to please someone else. Your ability to thrive may even be doing other people a favor. As they see you excel, they may be inspired by you to become better versions of themselves.

I would rather spend time alone than spend time with someone who is harmful to my spirit. If you walk with wise people, you will stack the cards in your favor. If you strap yourself to fools, you will watch your life crumble. Don't settle for second best. Surround yourself with people who are happy when you succeed, who inspire you to be your best self. Find people you admire, and if they're not readily available in your life, think of how you can connect with them.

Volunteering can help you find both like-minded people and a way to help others. I talk about this a lot in my book *A Dose of Tia*. I love animals, and I'm fascinated with the medical industry. In 2011, I began volunteering with my dog by taking her to visit staff and patients at our local hospital. This introduced me to so many wonderful and inspiring people on the hospital staff and in the Denver Pet Partners organization.

Perhaps you could ask someone at work or school if he or she could be your mentor. If you love playing basketball, join a league or coach a youth team. If you enjoy investing, join a club that meets on a regular basis so that you can learn from, collaborate with, and meet new people who have similar interests that inspire you. There are endless opportunities to help you match your interests to programs. Expose yourself to new activities, and you'll find like-minded and inspirational people.

YOU'VE GOT THIS:

If you hang around naysayers, you too will become a naysayer. If you spend your time challenging yourself and nurturing your soul, you will keep improving and moving forward.

CHAPTER 25

Introverts and Extroverts
Both Are Magnificent

P eople are different, which is a great thing! (Note the chapter on tolerance.) Initially, one way to categorize different personalities is by applying the "introvert" and "extrovert" groupings. For some reason, I find people tend to want to be an extrovert, as though that's the better of the two. This might be because extroverts seem to get more attention and appear more charismatic and happy, as if they're having the time of their lives. I, however, disagree. There is beauty in both extroverts and introverts.

Introverts look for a quiet space to reduce stimulation. They may seem antisocial, but they're not. They can be alone, but not feel lonely. Introverts can be completely content spending an entire Saturday by themselves doing what they love. However, introverts may need to be careful to recognize if they're becoming too isolated.

Because interacting can feel like work for introverts, they should ensure that they practice their social skills. Have a handful of questions at the ready: "How are...? Have you...? What if...?" These will help guide you in those awkward, panic-inducing moments when you don't know what to say but want to talk about more than the weather. If you employ conversational and social skills even when it feels like work, invitations won't be in short supply. Be a wallflower if you prefer, but be confident that with some effort and a moment's notice, you could be the life of the party.

Extroverts look for stimulation; they thrive on it and usually aren't comfortable alone. Extroverts repair themselves by being social, drawing energy from others. They tend to enjoy being the center of attention, and they usually are. Their challenge is that their emotions can be a rollercoaster ride; they're high and then low. If care isn't taken, an extrovert's life can feel hectic, bouncing between stimulations. Uncomfortable as it may seem, extroverts should integrate some downtime. No one and nothing can run 100 percent of the time.

One of my good friends is an extrovert, yet I am not. I had to put up boundaries because at times she became overwhelming for me. I was content in my quiet space, and she was continually and lovingly trying to pull me out of it. After a long talk one day, we agreed that we're just two dear friends working in slightly different worlds. We simply had to understand each other's makeup.

One day my doorbell rang. When I answered, she was on the doorstep with her dog, bird, and three kids.

"Jonathan is out of town," she said. "I knew you would make up an excuse, so I just came over. I just hate being alone." Then, she walked past me toward the family room.

I loved her honesty; at the same time, I could see how desperate she was to connect. Yes, she had animals and three children, but she didn't have an adult connection for the weekend. This made her feel hopeless enough to knock on an introvert's door. I loved that she felt comfortable enough with me to do this. So, as a friend, I was there for her. We understood each other.

Whether you fall within the introvert or the extrovert category, embrace and manage what you're made of. I wholeheartedly believe one isn't better than the other. Each has benefits and challenges. The key to being at peace with yourself is finding your social connection sweet spot. If you find yourself falling too deeply into introversion, employ your social skills and get to work. On the contrary, if the extrovert inside of you is running at 100 percent for too long, reel it in and recalibrate. Find the balance that feels right for you.

> **YOU'VE GOT THIS:**
> Respect, nurture, and repair your soul in a way that works uniquely for you.

CHAPTER 26

When You Feel Lonely

It breaks my heart to think of a loved one, or anyone, as lonely. However, loneliness is an emotion everyone has experienced, but few have truly acknowledged. Everyone is familiar with it, but few discuss it. Perhaps most of us don't know how to label what we're feeling. We might have a few hundred friends on social media, dozens of colleagues at work, a handful of classmates, some friends, and family, but we can still feel distant and alone.

We don't have to be alone to feel lonely. On the other hand, we can be completely alone and not feel lonely at all. Confusing?

It's all about connection. You may be surrounded by people at work, in the classroom, and at home, but if you don't feel connected, loneliness can creep in. Imagine you had a tough day at school, and then when you went to work, your computer crashed. Finally, when you got home, your family didn't understand why you were down. They didn't support you. This would create a sense of loneliness and disconnection within you.

Drastic life changes can also inflict a sense of loneliness. A death in the family, a friend struggling with mental illness, the loss of a job—all of these situations could catapult you into a world where you feel alone and isolated.

Once you're honest with yourself and label your feelings as loneliness, don't be ashamed. Be brave and authentic. You can't fix what you don't know. Also, realize that loneliness can play tricks on your mind and morph your reality to the point where your behavior shifts. When lonely, you are usually very insecure and sensitive. You may be hesitant to reach out to a friend who declined your invitation (even for a good reason), because you'd be devastated if she didn't respond again. Your loneliness would be compounded. Reaching out wouldn't be worth the gamble. If you didn't feel lonely, though, a rejection wouldn't hurt your feelings; you'd shrug it off and make plans to get together another day.

When you're lonely, you begin to build a brick wall to protect yourself from further emotional damage. This becomes a counterintuitive cycle. You're lonely, so you don't allow yourself to be vulnerable, so you become lonelier. This is the time when you need to dust yourself off and fight. Here is the place to dig in and do the work.

Below are some suggestions to combat loneliness:

1. When you feel helpless, help someone. Reach out to a friend who you know is struggling. Offer assistance or lend an ear.

2. Volunteer.

3. Discover optimism and realize that bad things are temporary.

4. Get some exercise.

5. Uncover your strengths. List them and put them to work for you.

6. Avoid toxic people and get involved in something, such as a club or class with like-minded, positive people.

7. When you hear that negative self-talk, realize that maybe you're wrong about yourself.

8. Smile at strangers. Nothing feels as good as making someone's day.

9. If you bump into a friend, give a hug. That way you get one too.

10. Engage, get out there, and participate in life.

You are not alone. You're never alone. This was written because someone else—many others—have gone through the same experiences. *You're magnificent. Get out there and share yourself with the world!*

YOU'VE GOT THIS:

You're brave to acknowledge and label your loneliness. Now is the time to share yourself, your mighty self, with the world.

CHAPTER 27

Making Someone's Day

Who doesn't love compliments? They are cheap to give, yet invaluable to the recipient, if they're authentic. How often do you examine people while they are speaking to you and notice something remarkable—how they look, dress, talk, or conduct themselves? Now consider this: how often do you verbalize what you are thinking?

At the grocery store one day, the woman scanning my items had the most stunning blue-green eyes I'd ever seen. They were such a rare color, like the shallow waters off a remote tropical island. While she continued to scan and my groceries slid past me, I wondered if she knew how beautiful they were. *Well, of course she does,* I told myself. *In fact, she's probably tired of hearing people comment on them.*

I decided I would compliment them anyway, even if it annoyed or distracted her.

"You're eyes are such a beautiful color," I said.

Stunned, she looked at me, and then her face lit up. She thanked me. From that moment on, she stood a little taller, her shoulders back, her face smiling. She seemed genuinely to glow.

In that moment, I learned that by giving an authentic compliment, I too reaped some benefits. I felt wonderful! I had made someone's day just by speaking my thoughts! It was so simple, but incredibly powerful.

Why do we keep our compliments to ourselves? They are so valuable to the people who receive them, but they don't cost a thing. Imagine how the world would change if everyone verbalized their positive thoughts.

Even if you don't actually compliment someone, you can help make their day a little brighter by simply noticing them. Did you even look in the eyes of the man who helped you choose your sneakers at the store? Do you know the name of the woman at your favorite restaurant? Even if you don't say a word, the simple act of noticing someone and smiling can positively influence that person's day.

YOU'VE GOT THIS:

Think of a time when someone complimented you and how that made you feel. Now is the time to give that gift to someone else.

CHAPTER 28

When Someone Is Grieving

Sometimes it's hard to know what to say or do when someone is grieving, especially a friend or family member. You might try to fix the pain, to make the other person laugh. Conversely, you may avoid that person in fear of saying or doing the wrong thing. These are all normal reactions.

My mother is a hospice volunteer who has seen good intentions displayed in all the right and wrong ways. Remember, each person grieves differently. Grief may involve extreme emotions and behaviors, and there is no set timeframe for how long it lasts.

Therefore, while you may have good intentions, you may not know what to say to a grieving person.

Communication can be touchy. Let's first talk about statements that you want to avoid.

1. "How are you?"
This makes the person feel pressure to adequately verbalize and relive their pain. If they feel comfortable, they will tell you this without prompting.

2. "I understand . . ." or "I know how you feel . . ."
Everyone feels and reacts differently; therefore, their loss is unique. Don't turn their pain into your story.

3. "He's in a better place . . ."
The fact is that he/she isn't here. That's what hurts.

4. "There is light at the end of the tunnel."
Grief must happen before they can feel the light. Let them grieve. Don't try to fix it prematurely.

In December 2014, my stepfather, Jim, passed away. Yes, he was almost ninety years old, but his health was impressive. He worked out every day, ate a healthy diet, had no addictions, and kept his mind active by doing daily puzzles. Quite simply, he defied the laws of science. So when suddenly he was hospitalized and two weeks later passed away, it was a shock to us. I will never forget a kind email I received from one of my closest and dearest colleagues.

Dear Dina,
I am so sorry for your loss and for what you are going through. When you have some time and you'd like to

talk, I would love to hear about all the ways Jim was special. I am here for you, to listen, to lend a shoulder to cry upon, and if you need to yell, I will listen to that too. I may not understand what you're going through, but I'm here for you, and I am thinking of you.

Although my heart was broken at that time, it was also full.

YOU'VE GOT THIS:
Often, you cannot take pain away, but you can give comfort by saying, "I am here for you."

CHAPTER 29

Navigating a Room Mostly Filled with Strangers

Don't fret. I'm here for you. You're not alone, and you can do this.

One cold December week, I was traveling for work to meet with hundreds of colleagues. Some I knew, but most I did not. On the first day, I was excited as the meetings unfolded, as I had a job to do and a function to perform. The hard part came in the evening, when we were expected to socialize at a cocktail reception for six hundred of my closest coworkers.

Minutes before entering the room, a pit formed in my stomach. Feeling like an oddball, silly and alone, I made my way to the door. Suddenly, an executive tapped me on my shoulder. "Do you mind walking in there with me?" she said. "I don't do well in these situations."

I was flabbergasted. Maybe I wasn't the only one who

felt this way. If anyone should have been able to navigate a crowded room, it should have been her, one of the most senior people there. She too, however, was a bit anxious to do it alone. I loved her honesty and authenticity. From that moment on, I have respected her more because of her candor.

So what should we do when we enter and navigate a crowded room?

1. Take a deep breath; at least 80 percent of the people there are just as nervous as you are.

2. Come prepared with topics to discuss or experiences to share.

3. Stand with open body language. Make eye contact.

4. Leave one hand free at all times. Don't check your phone out of nervousness or double up on plates or drinks.

5. Start by scanning the room and looking for someone else who is alone and seems welcoming. Introduce yourself.

6. Prepare a short elevator pitch as your introduction.

7. Compliment people. Be engaged when they talk.

8. Ask them about themselves. People love to talk about themselves.

9. Ask what they're excited about or what they're working on.

10. Note others' facial expressions and body language when deciding whether or not to approach them.

11. Look for opportunities to help others with information or introductions.

12. Look for eye contact or a nod from others as a signal to introduce yourself.

13. Ask for advice.

14. Talk about headlines, but no politics. Keep it positive.

15. Comment about the location/food/speaker/music. Keep it upbeat.

Here's what we shouldn't do:

1. Look over the shoulder of the person you're talking to as if someone more interesting may appear.

2. Try to overemphasize your expressions or look smarter or more boisterous to gain attention. People will see through this.

3. Get discouraged in the first ten minutes if things aren't going your way.

You can do this. Take a deep breath and build your confidence; your lack of it is your only enemy here. You're a fun, engaging, and interesting person—show everyone who you are. *They* are the fortunate ones to be able to interact with you!

YOU'VE GOT THIS:

A crowd is intimidating to almost everyone.
Employ the tools to help you shine—they're
fortunate you've joined them! Now, open the
door, stand tall, and smile.

CHAPTER 30

How You Fit into the Workforce
It's Not All about IQ

From an early age, we learned that excelling at reading, writing, and math would lead to a successful life. In elementary, middle school, and high school, our good grades were celebrated. Our marginal grades were often looked upon with disappointment, because it was assumed we didn't try hard enough. Sometimes, they were even looked upon with sorrow. Maybe someone wrongfully concluded we just weren't "smart enough." After working for over twenty years in one of the largest, most successful technology companies in the world, I'm here to tell you that it's not all about IQ.

Your IQ might get you in the game, but it won't predict how successful you'll be. Being the smartest person in the room may be most important in some professions, but in general, it's probably least important. What's critical instead are your emotional intelligence and grit, your determination.

Emotional intelligence is critical because being in the workforce is always a team venture. You need to be able to connect with people. Seeing things through other people's eyes is essential. Tune in to feeling how they are feeling (the *walk a mile* analogy). Paying attention instead of checking your cell phone while someone's talking is critical, as is developing a good rapport with your colleagues. If a supervisor or boss is hammering his employees with unrealistic deadlines, he won't have a team for long.

Grit, otherwise known as determination, may be the most useful measuring stick for success. Grit is about showing up and doing what needs to be done, about being dependable, and, when things go wrong, about persevering. Grit is about making those twenty-eight phone calls to get that one "yes." People with grit not only ensure that things don't fall through the cracks; they seal those cracks so that things never can. I once had a boss tell me he'd rather hire someone with a C average who has strong perseverance than a straight-A student who doesn't.

Once you're in the workforce, make sure you celebrate your accomplishment! You made this happen. Relish in your achievement even though you may look around and wonder if you fit in. Most people in the workforce sometimes feel like frauds, as though they don't have the credentials and they're faking it, even after decades. I recently heard of a famous musician who struggles with this. Who is this supposed fraud?

Paul McCartney, from the Beatles. He's a giant in the music business, worth half-a-billion dollars. His songs are idolized and enjoyed by people around the world from ages ten to 110. He'll be remembered as one of the greatest musicians of all time. And still, in an interview, he said he suffers with insecurity. He's afraid of "being found out," that one day he won't be able to fool people any longer.

We are all unique. Being successful in a profession isn't just about IQ, as we may have grown up to believe. Success is about human connection and determination.

Here is a list of my favorite "must-dos" on the job.

1. Be on time.

2. Be dependable and reliable.

3. Don't make excuses. Name challenges, but come up with suggestions to solve them.

4. Offer to help.

5. Put in the work and have pride in your output.

6. Bring good energy. Don't gossip, whine, or complain.

7. Your job is to make your boss's job easier. If he or she is chasing you down and/or listening to excuses, you're a burden.

8. You're not entitled to your job; you earn it. Your place of employment doesn't owe you anything other than a fair chance to excel if you put in the work.

9. Look beyond yourself and the bigger picture. Don't burn any bridges—you never know what the future may hold. You may end up looking smaller in the eyes of others.

10. Don't do anything to tarnish your brand or reputation. If you're bitter, upset, or angry, hit pause before you react.

11. Be careful of those motivational scenic posters with words in calligraphy such as *Fake it 'til you make it*. Set yourself up for success and have confidence you can do it, but also be authentic. Don't say you can do something that you can't. If you don't know something, tell them you'll learn it.

12. Look forward to growth. Be genuine, friendly, and approachable. You work with humans who have emotions. Make connections in an authentic way; work will seem less robotic and much more genuine.

CHAPTER 32

You Get What You Give

You're in control of what you get out of life. If accomplishments or things were given to you, you would neither appreciate nor respect them. I know what you're probably thinking: "If I lived in a mansion, having beer and gourmet hamburgers served to me poolside daily, life would be just great!" I disagree. This lifestyle might be terrific for the first few days or even weeks, but it would start to get old at the one-month mark. By then, you'd be asking yourself what *you* did to attain those luxuries. What did you accomplish that makes you proud of yourself?

Laziness and handouts are not on the path to a fulfilled life. Plain and simple, *you get what you give*. If you feel unfulfilled in an area of your life, be honest. Ask yourself, "What did I give in that area? How much did I contribute?"

For example, you may envy a friend's marriage, but how much effort have you poured into your own relationships? You may covet your sibling's international travels, but how hard have you worked to save money to travel yourself? If you want love, you first have to love. If you want respect, you first have to respect yourself.

Ninety-nine percent of the time, you get what you give. If you work out hard at the gym, your body will show it. If you allocate time to your studies, your grades will reflect your hard work. On occasion, you might put effort into a relationship, but the other person doesn't reciprocate. Move on. If there is something you truly want in life and you're not getting it, first realize that there is a better way. You are in control. Second, pay attention to the assignments on how to get what you want in life. Third, show up and do them.

When someone has something in his life that you covet, don't be bitter. Realize that he made it happen for himself. Be careful with your time. How you spend your time and the people you surround yourself with predict what your life will become. Don't hide behind electronics or numb yourself. Make choices today for which your future self will thank you.

> ### YOU'VE GOT THIS:
> There are no secrets to life. You get out what you put in. That, my dear, should give you peace, since you are in the driver's seat.

CHAPTER 33

Is He (or She) the One?

Love—undoubtedly, you have filled someone's heart and someone has filled yours. Tales are told of how great love has torn nations apart. Countless books, movies, poems, and websites are dedicated to looking for and finding love. However, I believe that you do not need to be married or in a committed relationship to feel complete.

I do understand that there's great pressure to find a partner. For instance, when summarizing who we are in a few words to a stranger, we usually feel the need to say whether or not we're in a relationship. However, this is one area where people should never take shortcuts or skimp. Some try to rush it, but deep, lifelong love is worth working and waiting for.

Therefore, if and when you do find someone, how do you know if he or she is "the one"? For me, this is what lifelong love looks like.

1. If you have to ask yourself *Are they the one?* then they likely aren't. If you are deeply in love, you have no question in your mind. Your heart can feel a deep, peaceful, and abiding love. It's like when you go shopping for a new shirt and try it on in the dressing room. If you look in the mirror and love the way it looks, you don't have to walk out to ask someone else's opinion. You just know it's right.

2. Love is when you're not afraid to tell someone you love him, as long as you really do. And I hope you do.

3. Love is when you choose to be at your best when your partner is not.

4. Love is when what you want isn't as important as what your partner wants. When both partners think like this, a beautiful flow of exchange is established.

5. Love is when you truly enjoy spending time together.

6. Love is when your heart and soul feel safe in your partner's hands.

7. Love is when you can trust your partner will always make decisions with you in mind.

8. Love is when you build each other up and have each other's back. If there is a disappointment, you are honest and work through it together.

9. Love is when you feel a sense of calm and euphoria when you see your partner for the first time after a week apart.

10. Love is mutual respect.

11. Love is when something great happens and your partner is the first person you think of to call and share the news with. When you do, your partner is truly happy for you.

12. Real love brings a sense of peace and calm. It moves freely between the two of you. You love each other as is, even the imperfections. You can help improve those imperfections in each other—you make each other better together.

13. Love doesn't mock, cut down, or belittle.

14. Love realizes that you and your partner are a team. If your partner thrives, so do you.

15. When you find lifelong love, it's usually quite obvious. You can feel it in your core.

YOU'VE GOT THIS:

Love—you know when it happens.

CHAPTER 34

Why Can't Everyone Be Like Me?
A Note on Tolerance

I don't care if you're gay, straight, black, white, Christian, Muslim, rich, or poor. If you're kind to me, I'll be kind to you. It's that simple.

When we speak about tolerance, we often think of the big subjects. What we often don't discuss are the smaller daily interactions during which our tolerance may be tested. The people in line in front of us may be covered in tattoos and piercings, or be dressed, let us say, uniquely. Perhaps, though, they're trying to tolerate us because we *don't* have tattoos. Who says that the way we do it (whatever "it" is) is the right way?

What about the baby crying on the airplane? Having three children, I feel for parents in this situation. They are usually doing everything they can to calm the child and are likely exhausted. Their day has just begun; a sleepless night awaits. *If your biggest problem in that moment is the slight annoyance of listening to their crying baby, then your life is tremendous.*

On a brisk Florida day, when I was a teenager, my mother was driving me to my orthodontist appointment. It was cool enough that we had our car windows down, a rare event in hot Florida. The breeze felt good. We stopped at a light. While we were waiting, a loud racket and pounding music began behind us, growing louder as a car pulled up next to us. It was a white, older model car decked out with spinning rims. The car sat low to the ground, had large fins in the back, and a green neon light underneath that made the road below it glow. The music was not to my taste; it was raucous, the bass kicking.

Aggravated, I rolled up my window. "Why do they have to be so annoying?" I said.

Very calmly, my mom replied, "If everyone were the same, it would be a pretty boring world."

The light turned green and we drove away to silence, but those words were loud and clear.

Sure, people can be annoying, but did their loud music really hurt me? They seemed to be enjoying themselves. I'm not suggesting that we pollute the earth with noise and infringe upon others, but sometimes we judge without knowing the full picture. See the beauty in others and try to be less judgmental.

YOU'VE GOT THIS:
If everyone were the same, it would be a
pretty boring world.

PART FOUR

Loving the Magnificent Journey

CHAPTER 35

Life Is about Courage

When I think of courage, I get an image of an armed Greek warrior, a firefighter saving a child from a burning building, or a US soldier confronting the enemy. Brave acts, however, aren't exclusive to situations like those. We can all be brave every single day. Being courageous is about doing what is necessary, even when it's hard. It's about showing up, doing the right thing, and being brave enough to be vulnerable.

- I believe you are brave when you respectfully stand up for what you believe and finally say what needs to be said.

- I believe you are brave when you put your heart out into the open and allow it to be vulnerable to the world.

- I believe you are brave when you say "no" when necessary.

- I believe you are brave when you ask for help.

- I believe you are brave when you open up to someone. (Just make sure that he or she has first earned your trust.)

- I believe you are brave when you find the gain in the pain.

- I believe you are brave when you allow yourself to be both soft and strong.

- I believe you are brave when you apply for that job.

- I believe you are brave when you put the work in to improving yourself.

- I believe you are brave when you allow yourself, your true self, to be seen.

- I believe you are brave when you set boundaries, but not brick walls.

- I believe you are brave when you no longer try to fit in.

You'll find that when you show your true self that people will be drawn in. This lesson came to me one night when my son had a sleepover. One particular boy in the group was a little quirky. That night, he pulled my son aside and told him that he always slept with the lights on and asked if we could leave them on for the sleepover. Of course, my son obliged; it was really no big deal.

The next day, after all the boys left, my son told me the story. At the end, he said, "I hope he knows I would never tell anyone." The boy who was brave enough to stay the night and vulnerable enough to expose his fears had earned my son's fierce protection. He had it from that day on.

When you open your heart and make the right, and often difficult choices, good things show up. If you put out into the world what is inside of you—your true self—things will fall into place. If you choose to hide, however, fear and uncertainty will likely destroy you.

YOU'VE GOT THIS:
Courage isn't about being hard; more often, it's about being soft.

CHAPTER 36

Sacrifices
Squeezing the Balloon

Your time is precious. Every second, minute, and hour that I sit writing this for my sons, I am dedicating time toward this one activity over another. Every minute we make decisions. Do I grab coffee or continue writing this report? Do I play basketball with the guys after work or have dinner with my girlfriend? Do I take the job overseas or stay close to family and friends? Do I forgo an immediate income by attending graduate school, or do I jump into the workforce? Do I go workout or sit on the couch and surf channels? Time is our most valuable resource, but often our most wasted, as it's sometimes invisible to us.

The *Merriam-Webster Dictionary* defines sacrifice this way: "the act of giving up something that you want to keep especially in order to get or do something else or to help someone." Essentially, we can't have it both ways. We'll all have to make larger choices that will ultimately mold our lives, and these choices almost always involve sacrifice. How important to you is having children or financial success? How will your career choice influence your daily life? For instance, if you choose to be in the military, you'll have a multitude of benefits, but if you have a family, the long-term deployments could be challenging.

Many years ago, I was on a flight coming home from a short work trip during Thanksgiving week. I sat next to a man who struck up a conversation. It turned out he was a senior referee for the NBA. As we talked, he was typing away, creating the schedule for the NBA referees. With all of his airline travel, I was surprised that he was in the cheap seats with me. He explained that he'd missed his flight, so this was his only option—next to me. Lucky guy.

I found his profession interesting, so naturally I began asking questions. Before long, we were knee-deep in an honest and heartfelt discussion. He explained that he had played basketball for a few years, but despite his efforts, he just wasn't good enough to stay in the NBA. Being a referee was the next best option.

I asked him where he was spending the holidays.

"On the road," he said.

At one point, he sat back and looked as though he was peering into his past. He told me of his youth. He described himself as the star basketball player in high school; in college, the NBA drafted him. As the talent of the players around him increased, his playing time decreased. He talked about how the lure of being an NBA star drew him in, but in hindsight, he questioned the sacrifices he'd made along the way. He would say, "Beware of the glitter in life." Short-term joys pull you in, but in the longer term—and in the bigger picture—they may lead you in the wrong direction.

As he spoke, I made a comment about his success. So few people have made it to such heights. He had been in the NBA! Smiling, he said, "Yes, I was . . . but not for long." He seemed proud of himself, but somewhat conflicted.

Life is a carefully crafted dance. When you step in one direction, you need to balance that decision with your next move. We can't always see the outcome of our choices and sacrifices, but we can try to focus on the bigger picture. We can try to imagine how a big decision is likely to play out. Always be one step ahead. Your choices, which are ultimately sacrifices, will impact your next move.

When you give your attention to one thing, you'll naturally have less to focus on another. Like a balloon being squeezed, your attention will bulge on one end and narrow at the other. In this referee's case, he was living a professional life many would envy, but his personal life was being squeezed out. If he was content and at peace with his sacrifices, then he would know he had made the right decisions for himself. In the end, you too will want to be content and at peace. If you're moving in the wrong direction, it's never too late to correct your path.

YOU'VE GOT THIS:

Every day, every minute you are making choices and sacrifices. Be conscious that those choices are moving you in the direction of your dreams.

CHAPTER 37

Challenge Yourself and Have a Plan

Challenge myself? That sounds hard. When do I get to relax? When does life get easy?

I know, I know—sitting around with no deadlines, appointments, or commitments seems ideal, but downtime is only temporary. We all need rest, but if we remain stagnant, we will wither away.

This may be hard to hear, but life isn't about a big break or handouts. It's about owning where you are and getting to where you want to go—one step at a time. Those who get the big breaks too soon often aren't equipped to handle them. Good, long-lasting things in life take time and commitment; they're worth fighting for. If they were easy, everyone would have them.

Take control of your destiny. You are either going to choose for yourself or have to accept what falls upon you when you don't take action. Don't wait for things to get easier, simpler, or better. Life will always be complicated. Learn to be happy right now and make a plan that moves you toward fulfillment. Trust me; it's worth it.

When you are making wrong choices, you know it inside. You hear your inner voices: "Get up from the couch" or "Make that phone call." The *real you* reminds you of the person you are supposed to be. One day you may no longer be able to rely on others to give you that loving nudge, so listen to the *real you*, even when ignoring it may seem easier.

I believe that many people walk around in a mental fog, seemingly half-asleep. Devotion to friendship, love, and self-fulfillment will awaken you. When you were a toddler, you beamed; you had that spark in your eye. Over the years, that childhood glow can be dulled in everyone. So tap into that magic, into that flicker, and be alive in your life. The world needs your unique self.

Being proactive and working hard catapult you forward. A sense of peace grows inside of you, as well as self-esteem and confidence. Taking the easy path is boring. You get what you give. For instance, if you eat healthy and exercise, you'll feel better, and it will show.

Be inspired by others who excel. There are no shortcuts in life. (Dang it!) Today's choices are tomorrow's reality.

1. Make big goals, but also make smaller milestones to get you there.

Celebrate your accomplishments, big and small, along the way! Go ahead—do something you love. Reward yourself in a healthy way. This will help keep you going. One of my neighbors is an inspirational, confident, and strong eighty-eight-year-old woman. Every day she sets small goals and achieves them. She does a sit up for every year of her life. She reads the paper, but doesn't let the headlines bring her down. She honors her passion for gardening by planting new flowers. By sticking to her goals, she thrives and moves forward.

2. Never stop improving.

Life rewards action. In order to survive, a shark must always move forward, pushing water through its gills so that it can breathe. You must do the same. Don't ever become stagnant—*keep going.*

YOU'VE GOT THIS:
Trust in yourself. Invest in the right people and put in the work— it will all pay off.

CHAPTER 38

Twelve Tips for Holding onto Happiness

I want you to be happy; more important, you deserve to be happy. Everyone deserves to be happy! The amount of happiness in the world has no limits. By experiencing joy yourself, you're not taking away from other people. In fact, you're inspiring them to find their own joy.

Often when things were going well, I was afraid to feel true joy. I feared that if I let my guard down, I would become blind and weak. How often have you been afraid to celebrate something wonderful because you thought the rug might be pulled out from under you and you'd come crashing down to reality? I fell into this trap numerous times until I learned to lean into happiness and feel it fully.

Be full of thanks. If you are getting married, feel that warmth and joy. Don't reduce your experience because you're afraid of being hurt. Why live a limited life? Live a joyful, grateful one.

1. Invest in valuable relationships.

2. Be in charge and own your happiness. Don't rely on others to give it to you or say, "I'll be happy when . . ."

3. Don't bring your past into the future. Chances are that you're too hard on yourself and have negatively morphed the reality of your past. This life is *your* story—if you don't like the past, rewrite it!

4. Dedicate time to yourself and *for* yourself. You yourself are a project—self-improve and self-repair.

5. Lose yourself in a variety of music that you love.

6. Enjoy the journey and don't just focus on the destination. Celebrate milestones large and small.

7. Protect your work/life balance. If you dedicate too much time to one, the other will suffer. Happiness and fulfillment come from moving forward through progress (work) *and* enjoyment (life).

8. Guard your mind and nurture it. Keep toxic information and people out.

9. Don't be afraid to laugh hard and laugh out loud.

10. For even a few minutes at least twice a day, be fully present in the moment. Notice what's happening around you. Put away the tech devices and distractions.

11. Find a role model who shows you what's possible.

12. For thirty to sixty minutes a day, strengthen your body. Stress, fear, and anger are physical and need to be released.

YOU'VE GOT THIS:

What is the secret to a happy life? There is no secret. You get out of life what you put into it. Happiness doesn't just show up on your doorstep. Happiness is a discipline, a practice.

CHAPTER 39

Three Tips for Managing Worry

believe males and females worry in different ways. Females are a bit more transparent, usually verbalizing their worry or somehow acting out. Men or boys tend to internalize worry, experiencing their anxiety in a quieter fashion. Either way, worry can be a depleting, useless anchor.

I always thought that if I worried about something, I had my eye on it so that it couldn't creep up on me. I would worry about my performance at work. I would worry about getting a strange superbug that was just on the news. I would worry about an accident while flying. I had it in my mind that if I kept those things front and center, I would be best prepared if they happened. I wouldn't make the mistake of being naïve to the dangers in the world. I was on it.

What I didn't realize was how much energy and anxiety I was wasting on worrying about unlikely events. Today, the media (social and not) feeds on fear. If it's an online headline, they want to make you click on the article so that they can make more advertising money. If they get your attention, their ratings go up.

Here is an example of a headline: "This Common Kitchen Utensil Almost Killed This Ohio Man." It panics you. *Holy smokes! I need to read this! If I don't, I could be in danger, and it's my own fault if I'm not aware!* A more truthful headline would have been "Ohio Man Cut Himself in the Kitchen by Accident." However, would you have read that article?

Be aware of these tactics. Before social media and the ratings wars, information was shared only if it was important to your life. An Ohio man cutting his finger is not newsworthy, but a twisted version of the story can seem scary enough to pull you in.

My neighbor is a wise eighty-eight-year-old woman born in the Czech Republic. She's vibrant, strong, and positive. One morning, I asked her if she worried about all the violence and shootings on the news lately.

She looked at me as if I had three heads. "Why would I do that? Look, I'm eighty-eight. I have seen so much, but if I had worried about whether or not those things would happen, I would have wasted years of my life. No, I don't worry."

Worry is such a wasteful act. In fact, it's worse than that. The more time you spend thinking about something (failing at your job or getting cancer), the more your tricky brain begins to seduce you, pulling you in. Soon, your mind is fixated on anxiety; it can't distinguish fact from fiction.

Some level of worry is productive, but most is not. Try these three tips for managing your worries.

1. Problem solve; don't worry.
If there's a true problem ahead of you, figure it out and take action. If no action can be taken, worry is wasteful.

2. Delay or reschedule your worry time.
Write it down and tell yourself you'll do it later. This is effective because you're acknowledging your worry and putting it aside. Soon it will dissipate. This also gives you an opportunity to review what you wrote down each week. When you reflect back, you may begin to see a wasteful pattern of worrying about things that never occurred.

3. Use the talk-to-someone test.
If you're hesitant to talk your worry through with a confidant, maybe it's because you realize it's wasteful.

YOU'VE GOT THIS:
Imagine your ninety-year-old self. Now add up all the months and years you spent on useless worries throughout your life. How much time did you waste?

CHAPTER 40

Out of the Nest and Certainly Not Falling
Nine Tips for College Freshman

Congratulations, graduate! I know high school can encapsulate every possible range of emotion. The pendulum swings from incredible and fun to gut wrenching and challenging. The great experiences solidified your confidence; the difficult experiences helped make you more resilient. No matter what your experience may have been, it built you up and laid the foundation for a better version of yourself.

Going off to college is a major life shift. For some, it's scary; for others the date can't come soon enough. Regardless of where you stand on the spectrum, you are loved, and you are fortunate. Nine key things can help you maximize your college experience.

1. **Connect.**

   • Engage with people in class. Promote a group study session.

   • Leave your dorm room open during the day as much as possible.

   • Limit texting, especially as you walk around campus. Make eye contact.

2. **Respect your body, mind, and health.**

   • Eat well. Sleep enough.

   • Stay active!

   • Avoid risky behavior such as drinking, smoking, drugs, and casual sex.

3. **Show up and engage.**

   • Take Woody Allen's advice: 80 percent of success is just showing up.

   • Sit in the middle or front of the lecture hall or classroom. A dear friend of mine who is a professor claims that those who sit in the back almost always get the worst grades.

   • Engage in discussion. The class likely can benefit from what you have to say.

   • Put in the effort.

4. **Reach out and tap into resources.**

   • Leverage your professors' office hours.

- If an essay or report is due, show them your draft and get their input.

- When you see or meet with your professors or TAs, introduce yourself and remind them of your name.

5. **Leverage campus life.**
   - Leverage all that your campus has to offer—intramural sports, clubs, events, groups, and gatherings.

6. **Consider a study abroad program.**
   - Once you graduate and need to find a job to pay back your loan, travelling to other countries might be much more challenging.

7. **Be your own best advocate.**
   - College is a huge step. If you're feeling uncomfortable, don't go it alone. Reach out. Your trusted family and friends are still your support system.

8. **Be wise and crafty with your money.**
   - College may seem like an eternity, but one day you will leave it behind and have to face your spending habits.

9. **Have fun!**
   - Oh, but not *too* much fun. ☺

YOU'VE GOT THIS:
Tuck these pages inside your suitcase and visit them often. I'm always here for you within these words. You're already a superstar!

CHAPTER 41

Ten Ways to Get Through Your First Day, Week, and Month on the Job

You've made it! It's your first job after graduating, and now you're expected to act like a grown up. In some ways, you may feel like a fraud, still a student, just better dressed. Here's the deal—unless you're a doctor, engineer, or in another profession where calculations are critical, your new company doesn't really care what your grades were. It's true that grades are a reflection of your effort and ability, but what's important now is your grit, your ability to dive in, learn, and get back up when you make a mistake.

1. Ask questions!
You may be inclined to listen and be quiet. You may not want to bring too much attention to yourself. That's just fine, but asking questions is critical. You're not expected

to know the what/how/when of the business. The important thing is to be a sponge. Also, don't act like you know the answer. We can see through that. We're not concerned that you don't know the answer. We're only concerned you won't be willing to learn. And, if you aren't brave enough to ask questions, learning will take you a really long time.

2. At this point, your job is to make your boss's job easier.

If you're making excuses and/or not contributing, your manager will hear about it and that will make his or her life more difficult. Anticipate what he or she needs and send it before it's requested. Proactively provide a weekly report. This will keep you on track too.

3. Don't hide.

Everyone needs to decompress sometimes, but you should engage with peers and people in other departments. When you see them in the halls, greet them by name. Consider the rule that you won't eat alone more than three days a week. Even if you bring your lunch (which is admirable!), sit with people in the cafeteria or outside.

4. Bring positive energy.

Don't be lethargic. We all have days where we'd rather be somewhere else, but for the most part, be conscious of the type of energy you bring to calls, meetings, and conversations.

5. Develop your personal brand/reputation.

Since you're fresh on the job, you have a somewhat clean slate. Who are you? What do you want people to think of you? Just as different colas have brands, people have a personal brand. Think of friends or mentors. What is their brand? What resonates when you think of them or hear their name? Are they reliable? Trustworthy? Hard working? Authentic?

Everyone has a brand they develop and need to maintain. Just like a product, once the brand is tarnished, it's very difficult (but not impossible) to repair. What do you want people to think of when they hear your name? What will be your brand or reputation?

6. Keep your personal excuses in check.

Make as few excuses as possible. If you use one, it had better be authentic. Being both reliable and dependable is critical. When you do have a valid excuse for being late (like a flat tire), acknowledge that you inconvenienced people and apologize.

7. Never gossip, whine, or complain.

If there is an issue, bring it up and offer a possible solution. Gossip is never okay. If you talk about someone, the person receiving the information will assume you will talk about him or her too. Gossip breaks down trust on all fronts.

8. If you're late for a deadline, let them know in advance.

Don't just apologize. Acknowledge the inconvenience you've caused the other person. Don't simply send the report in late. Proactively communicate: "If it's okay with you, my report will be two hours late today because I want to get you the most accurate data, and I'm waiting on final numbers." Later, follow up with a note: "The report is attached. Thank you for your patience."

9. That awkward hallway march.

Eventually a long hallway will separate you from a coworker. He'll be too far away to talk with just yet, so you'll walk toward each other for fifteen to twenty seconds. This can be uncomfortable and awkward to cope with. Being in corporate America for close to twenty-five years, I've seen it all. Some people look at you the entire time. I find that slightly creepy. Some people look at you and then away; once you approach, they pretend to suddenly notice you and say hello abruptly. Some people look down at their phones and pretend they're very busy and important.

Here's what I would suggest. Look at them, make good eye contact, and then look away for a while. When they're close, make genuine eye contact again and state their name in your greeting. This is your opportunity to show confidence, make an impression, and be remembered. Don't hide behind your phone or slink.

10. Be on time.

Scratch that. Arrive a minute early.

YOU'VE GOT THIS:

A company or organization is investing in you. Show them they made a great choice!

CHAPTER 42

Decision-Making 101

Should I or shouldn't I? The decision-making process may take many forms: flipping a coin, rock-paper-scissors, or pulling a choice from a hat. What if the decision, however, is too important to leave up to chance?

Here are a few tips and tricks I've employed to help me make decisions.

1. Never, ever make a decision based on fear.
If we let fear drive our decisions, we are never going to feel pure joy. We won't know if we made the right choice. Take emotions out and drive with logic.

2. Pretend you are advising a friend in your position.
What would you suggest he do? This can be hard because

you have to step outside yourself and be nonjudgmental. Set aside some quiet time. Truly and carefully consider what advice you'd give to a friend.

3. Imagine you've already made a choice.

Let's say you're having a hard time choosing between job A and job B. Pretend for thirty minutes (and truly believe it!) that you chose job A. After the thirty minutes, what does your gut tell you? Write down what you're feeling. Give yourself time to reset and recalibrate.

Now pretend in the same fashion that you chose job B. What does your gut tell you? How do you feel? I find this an effective way to make a choice. Many times, you know inside what you need to do, but a variety of factors can cloud your judgment. This method goes right to your gut, which is usually dead-on.

4. List the pros and cons.

This is a typical way to reach a decision, but you can make it more informative by assigning a value to each pro or con. Use a number scale such as one (least impactful) to ten (most impactful) to weigh your pros and cons. Add up the scores, and see what they tell you.

5. Put it aside.

Yes, it seems counterintuitive to stop focusing on the decision-making process, but many times you need some distance from the problem. I'm not implying that you should procrastinate, but sometimes we need a clear mind to make our choice. Put the decision aside for a while and things will fall into place slowly and subconsciously. Once some time has passed, think through your options; the right choice may now seem clear.

YOU'VE GOT THIS:

Sometimes, many times, the answer is already inside of us. We just need to tune in to hear it.

CHAPTER 43

Technology and Unsocial Media

You are incredible and remarkable. No device, screen, or two-dimensional relationship can outweigh what you have to offer. Over the past thirty years, tremendous progress has been made by adding computers, laptops, smartphones, digital readers, and countless other gadgets to our lives. I remember when we first started using email at work. Initially, it was a little odd and hard to follow, so it wasn't fully embraced. Using email seemed like passing notes around the office via our large, clunky machines. Now, it is by far our primary means of communication. It's hard to imagine working any other way.

Technology pulls us together, helps us reconnect with friends across the globe, makes us more efficient, reduces paper waste, and stores much of our life on a teeny-tiny hard drive. Technology can even help us find and rekindle love. Like a magic genie, with a stroke of the keyboard, it grants us almost any information, twenty-four hours a day.

Technology has advanced our culture more quickly than any other tool or mechanism. However, anything used to an extreme or to replace fundamental human connection can pull you down and out-of-balance.

In 2016, we went on an amazing Alaskan cruise. As we watched the majestic landscape through the large windows, my family and I talked. At a table next to us, a middle-aged mother and father were both on their phones. Perhaps they needed to help a friend in crisis or knock out some work emails. Every few minutes their young children came up and tugged on the mother's sleeve.

"Mom, Mom! Look at me jump into the pool! Look!" they said. When they turned and ran to the pool enthusiastically, however, the mother never even looked up from her phone. That made me sad. She was there, but she wasn't really there. Of course, we all need to check our phones occasionally, but our devices have become both a crutch and a cloak to hide behind.

On another occasion, we were visiting friends who were hosting a small party. We were all out by the pool. As I glanced at the table where the teenage kids were sitting, I noticed that 80 percent of them were on their phones. They weren't engaging, talking with one another, or even making eye contact. They were avoiding the social situation by ducking behind their screens.

When I take my sons to appointments, many parents in the waiting room are on their devices as they sit next to their child. I get it: sometimes it's hard to put the device down and interact. If you don't, though, you're missing out on subtle learning opportunities. Being present in the moment and connecting is one of the most important contributors to human health and longevity.

One could argue that social media can fall into the category of being social. After all, you're connecting and communicating with other people! I believe social media can be both positive and negative. When people are authentic and kind, social media is a wonderful tool. However, when people post what they don't have the courage to say in person, social media is damaging.

When you engage with someone in person, you will notice her facial expressions, body language, and energy. When a few words show up on your screen, all of that is lost. You're left connecting with a cold, mechanical device through which people communicate quite differently than they do in person. Social media can quickly become *unsocial* media.

It seems we have so much more drama today than ever before because of social media. Our minds weren't created for encountering negativity, finger pointing, and bullying through a computer screen. When you take a break from technology, silence the voice in your head, and let go of trauma, you can move to the space where we are all the same, universally.

Technology *is* a marvel to me, and it has brought such progress to this world. However, we need to be careful that it never replaces the true human connection of face-to-face communication and compassion. Fiercely guard how you choose to spend your time; you are a dynamic, magnificent person who has so much to offer. Share yourself with this world and protect what you bring into your life, your mind, and your heart.

YOU'VE GOT THIS:
Nothing can replace a three-dimensional relationship that gives you eye contact, warmth, and a beating heart.

CHAPTER 44

Tips and Tricks to Avoid Procrastination

Procrastination reminds me of a rose—it's mesmerizing, but prickly.

We all procrastinate to a degree, but some allow it to affect their life and productivity. They dread doing something, so they put it off. Before long, it's a heavy backpack they're carrying around. Procrastination can ultimately drag your mood, confidence, and focus to the ground. It's a weight you want to shed as fast as possible.

Here are a few tips to rid yourself of that unwanted weight and find a more productive way to focus your mind.

1. Identify procrastination as soon as it creeps in.
This gives you the best chance of defeating it.

2. Always, always, always do the toughest task of the day first thing in the morning.

This will free up your mind and build confidence. If you dread calling your boss and telling him you're going to be late on a deadline, do it first. Delaying it will only be a burden on your shoulders and sour your day unnecessarily. You need to make the call, so get it over with. Try it once. The payoff might surprise you!

3. If it takes less than five minutes to do, do it right away.

No delays.

4. Understand why you're procrastinating.

If it's because the task is unpleasant, do that task right away and as quickly as possible. If it's because you are disorganized, see the section "Staying Neat and Organized." Once you can see order in your day and make a list, you'll be able to chip away at what you need to do. Finally, some people procrastinate because they feel overwhelmed by a big project; they just don't know where to start. In this case, break the project into small pieces, identify tiny milestones, and tackle the very first one, and then the next. Each small accomplishment will build your confidence, and you'll begin to see a light at the end of that long tunnel.

Procrastination is a self-induced burden that can be life altering. If it gets out of control, some might self-soothe to cope, and this can spiral into other areas of your life. If you despise doing taxes so much that on January first of each year you start to feel a weight on your shoulders, you may find yourself heading for a bag of chips. If so, identify the problem. Break up January through April 15 into acceptable, bite-sized chunks. Stick to this manageable schedule to tackle your taxes. Once you start checking milestones off your list and see the benefits of proactive behavior, you just might leave that bag of chips alone.

YOU'VE GOT THIS:
Procrastination is shortsighted; the pitfalls outweigh the benefits. As Nike® says, "Just Do It!"

CHAPTER 45

What a Magnificent Mess!
Staying Neat and Organized

Organizational skills come naturally to some people but not so much to others. Being organized isn't just about having a neat junk drawer and no clothes laying around the house. When you're truly organized, you're more efficient, better prepared, and much less stressed out. You show up to commitments equipped and on time. Being well organized also builds your self-confidence; fewer bombshells go off in your life, and if they do, you're likely better prepared for them.

I have three primary tools to keep me organized.

1. Email
We all get a lot of emails. Create folders, sort, and keep your inbox as clean as possible. If you have an action item,

put it on your daily to-do list, then file your email. Stay on top of this. Don't let your email get so out of control that you can't distinguish between what's important and what's not.

2. Daily to-do list

Make a list every day. Whether you feel more comfortable using paper/pen or an electronic notepad, do your best to check off items as you accomplish them. If you don't, push the item to the next day's list to complete.

Some days, the list might have only one thing on it—*relax*—and that's important too. Just because you have a list doesn't mean you have to accomplish everything on it. It shouldn't be intimidating. Be realistic about what you think you can do in a day. If you are ambitious, maybe you will get through the list and even do a few things you planned for the next day. If things are busy, move a few items to tomorrow. The list is there to scan several times each day so that you can continually prioritize.

Also, consider a weekend list. Print it out and place it on your counter for reference throughout the weekend. The following list might seem overwhelming, but the total time it takes to do each chore only consumes a small portion of the day. By putting tasks and activities down on paper, you eliminate the voice in your head.

☐ Mow yard

☐ Meet friends at Yard House Restaurant, 5 p.m.

☐ Grocery shop

☐ Check in on Mom

☐ Pack for work trip (see list of items to pack)

If you have a grocery list, Christmas gift list, or packing list for an upcoming trip, put them some place accessible so you can easily add items as they occur to you. Nothing is more exhausting than trying to remember a multitude of details. Take these details out of your mind and put them on paper. Free up your most valuable resource—your brain.

3. Calendar

Your calendar should include appointments and time to work on projects. When you have a meeting or appointment, don't just block off the start time, build in travel time, too. I find that those who are usually late don't build in transitional or travel time, adding to their habitual tardiness and stress.

☐ 10:30 – prepare for meeting (15 min.)

☐ 10:45 – walk to building #2 for meeting

☐ 11:00 – Product Management meeting

☐ 1:00 – work on new project

The more you can wrap your arms around your calendar, lists and emails, the less anxious you will be. You'll be better equipped for what's ahead of you. Feeling worried and restless is exhausting, drawing your energy away from more valuable areas of focus.

Be dependable. When you say you're going to do something, do it. Be consistent. Being otherwise will affect your relationships and self-esteem.

Just as some struggle to be organized, not everyone is neat and tidy. I believe being tidy is just as important as being organized. You could probably list a few people you know whose house or car are cluttered and messy. Perhaps *you* are that person.

Remember, your environment reflects how you feel on the inside. If you are unorganized, disheveled, and frantic, you can't have a peaceful existence. Walking into a neat and clean room just makes you feel better.

Being tidy and organized will help you take control of your life and destiny. How can you be proactive when you're overwhelmed by mounds of laundry and a discouraging pile of dishes in the sink? When you're organized, negative energy can't boil up and defeat you. Surround yourself with beauty and inspiration. Imagine a clean and organized life, home, car, and desk. Feel your self-respect rise.

Sometimes it helps to start small. Clean out your car and work on the discipline to keep it that way. After you begin to feel the beneficial effects, move to your bedroom, and then another room in the house. Before you realize it, you will be reaping the benefits of a clean and orderly environment. The payoff will outweigh the work.

I'm not implying you need a spotless home, but I do believe a messy, dirty and/or cluttered environment can be somewhat, if unconsciously, defeating. People feel a sense of joy and pride when they're surrounded by order. Create a home that gives you a sense of relaxation and pride when you walk in.

Just as you're thoughtful about whom you spend your time with, be thoughtful about your surroundings. When you have self-respect for your belongings and environment, you can reallocate and pour your energy into building your beautiful life.

> ### YOU'VE GOT THIS:
> If you map out your day and tidy up your environment, you'll sit in your beautiful space with a sense of calm and a little more self-respect.

CHAPTER 46

Knowing What's Important and Good

We spend so much time comparing and calculating how much we have versus how much they have, or we ruminate over what we think we want in life. As a result, we lose sight of the real markers of success. A core set of values and behaviors keeps us happy. If we lose our foundation, our happiness sits upon a pile of shifting and unstable sand, waiting for a wave to wash it all away.

If we focus on these core areas, we have a strong foundation that can hold a castle—our magnificent life.

1. Take care of your health, mind, and body.

2. Love and respect yourself—self-esteem.

3. Invest in valuable relationships.

4. Find purpose and fulfillment in your daily life.

5. Forgive. You don't forget, but you release the burden.

I recently spent time with my wise eighty-eight-year-old neighbor. I asked her how she thought people are different today from when she grew up. She told me that people have different priorities now. They want more "things;" they are less connected and helpful to each other. When she grew up, success meant happiness, contentment, and fulfillment. Today, people tend to measure success by material things, which may not bring them happiness. Successful movie stars, business men/women, and athletes in their prime often develop addictive and numbing behaviors, such as drinking, doing drugs, and gambling. Contrary to how they appear on the outside, they don't "have it all." Despite their material possessions and myriad of "yes people," they are still in some way unfulfilled and empty.

How much time do you daydream about an expensive home, car, trip, or clothing? How much time do you spend watching television or movies in which these items are glamorized? Conversely, how much focus do you place upon your health, self-love, relationships, or self-fulfillment? We are bombarded hourly with messages that money and luxury are what we should strive toward, but if you struggle with your health, would you really be happy in that luxury car? Would you trade that car to be pain-free?

I'm not implying that you can't have it all. I believe you can! You can have all of the health, wealth, and happiness life can offer, but not if any of your core values are absent. You can do without the yacht, but you cannot be happy when self-respect and self-love are missing. Start with the foundation and build your own castle. You'll be okay as long as you never lose sight of your values.

Too many times, we wallow in the bad and give it too much attention. Celebrate the good stuff, even the small milestones! By celebrating the milestones, you'll find it's easier to take a step forward. Each step forward is a step closer to your goal. For example, suppose you got the job you wanted after four months of trying. Yes, it's time to celebrate, but what about all the milestones that got you there? To search for available jobs, you created and revised your resume. You reached out to friends and old colleagues. You went on countless interviews and followed up afterward.

A lot of work goes into meeting a goal. By celebrating each one even in a small way, you'll inspire yourself to stay motivated. By toasting to your finished resume or by calling friends or family to share good news about an interview, you'll feel propelled to tackle the next step.

Momentum keeps us going, but once it stops, our goals are in jeopardy. People are sometimes afraid to be joyful. They fear that they might become stagnant and stop moving forward if they're happy. The exact opposite is true. A happy and fulfilled life expands your world and the possibilities within it. You meet new and different people. You try new things. You feel new emotions.

Don't stop and wait for good things to happen. Celebrate your life and your small accomplishments. Keep life's momentum moving you in the direction of your dreams.

YOU'VE GOT THIS:

When you focus on the important things in life and celebrate the milestones, it's easier (and oh, so much more fun!) to keep chugging up that glorious, awe-inspiring, jaw-dropping mountain.

CHAPTER 47

You Are Anything but Ordinary

You, my dear, are far from average or commonplace. You are extraordinary. You are a magnificent, unique individual who has the capacity to change this world for the better. We are all distinctive—every one of us—and that's what makes us anything but average.

Imagine your favorite candy bar. What is more important to you, the carefully crafted, consumer-focused marketing on the wrapper or the delicious, mouthwatering succulence of the candy bar itself? We are too hard on ourselves. We often compare ourselves to what we see as the complete and polished product of another person, whereas in reality, we're only looking at the packaging. Someone might be extraordinary at something that you're not, but you don't see the faults inside the lovely wrapper; you're only enamored by its sparkle.

So why do we allow ourselves to feel less than ordinary? I think we often fall into this trap when faced with other peoples' countless accomplishments and accolades; we start to feel "less than." Remember, those accomplishments are only a small fraction of what that person is made of. Just like you, they have a multitude of layers.

Instead of trying to be extraordinary at just one thing, follow your curiosity, dabble, and try new things. You'll connect with new people who have the same interests. You'll find comfort in a new variety of accomplishments and begin to feel the rhythm and purpose of life.

Nothing great comes from a lack of effort and discipline. You may not be the best at something, but you can always find your best life when you keep moving forward. You are magnificent—let your inner sweetness shine!

YOU'VE GOT THIS:

I once heard that it's more dangerous for a bird to be stagnant than to be flying. Don't hold yourself down. Just like a magnificently engineered bird, you were born to soar.

FINAL THOUGHTS

You are the author of your life; give the pen to no one else. Don't accept or get stuck in a "should have" life: I "should have" gone for my dream job or hit my goals. I "should have" married my love or climbed that mountain.

Consider a large sprawling oak tree. Because it is not visible like its branches, the tree's root system is underappreciated. After all, the roots, those underground tentacles, are the source of health or illness for the tree. They serve as an anchor against the wind and a lifeline for nutrients. Just as these invisible roots are the foundation for the tree, the work you do on the inside must strengthen your own foundation. Keep your root system stable, strong, and healthy. When the winds of life stress your core, your internal unwavering grit will serve as your strength.

Only the stories and the voices in our heads limit us. You always have the power. Focus on you. When you're strong, confident, and contributing to life, everything else will fall into place. Failure is only information telling you to dust yourself off and get back up. Be authentic. Be all in. Stand tall and try again.

Some people will give good advice, but some people won't. You must learn to distinguish between the two. You will know in your gut when the advice is sound. Good things in life take a long time and a lot of effort. They're worth fighting for. If they came easily, everyone would have them; they'd no longer be special.

Whether you're heading off to college, going on job interviews, starting over in a new city or taking time for yourself, figure things out. We're all works in progress. The magnificence of life is that there is no shortage of health, happiness, and fulfillment. Everyone can enjoy a brilliant existence without ever detracting from someone else. In fact, your happiness can be a source of inspiration for others. Just like an oak tree, whose roots can total hundreds of miles and even graft together with other oaks, your strength can support healthy growth in other people. It all starts with your personal, thriving root system.

Your magnificent life awaits—you can do this!

ABOUT THE AUTHOR

Dina Mauro has worked in the technology industry for over twenty-five years, twenty with one of the world's largest high-tech companies. Through her love for animals, Dina began rescuing dogs, volunteering, and, ultimately, writing.

Dina is the author of *A Dose of Tia: How a Woman and Her Rescued Dog Embraced Life Through Volunteering – and How You Can, Too.* Initially, as a personal, heartfelt gift to her sons, but later published for the public, Dina went on to pen *You've Got This! The Grad's Guide to the Big, Rich, Magnificent Life You Deserve.*

She also volunteers at Denver Pet Partners, Swedish Medical Center, and Children's Hospital Colorado, along with her three sons.

Dina lives in Denver with her husband, Bob, and their three sons, Owen, Ethan, and Aiden.